REALITY TELEVISION

The Television Phenomenon That Changed the World

RUTH A. DELLER
Sheffield Hallam University, UK

emerald
PUBLISHING

United Kingdom – North America – Japan – India
Malaysia – China

Emerald Publishing Limited
Howard House, Wagon Lane, Bingley BD16 1WA, UK

First edition 2020

Copyright © 2020 Ruth A. Deller

Published under an exclusive license

Reprints and permissions service
Contact: permissions@emeraldinsight.com

British Library Cataloguing in Publication Data
A catalogue record for this book is available from the British
Library

ISBN: 978-1-83909-024-0 (Print)
ISBN: 978-1-83909-021-9 (E-ISBN)
ISBN: 978-1-83909-023-3 (Epub)

ISOQAR certified
Management System,
awarded to Emerald
for adherence to
Environmental
standard
ISO 14001:2004.

Certificate Number 1985
ISO 14001

INVESTOR IN PEOPLE

In memory of Diane Kershaw (1970–2016), who introduced me to Strictly Come Dancing and always wanted my first book dedicating to her.

CONTENTS

ABOUT THE AUTHOR

Ruth A. Deller is a Reader in Media and Communication at Sheffield Hallam University. She has published widely on a range of topics including: reality and factual television; fan and audience studies; media representations of gender and religion; and more. She is on the editorial board of *Celebrity Studies* journal and has edited special issues of *Sexualities* (with Bethan Jones and Sarah Harman) and the *International Journal of Cultural Studies* (with Feona Attwood).

PREFACE

Reality television is arguably the defining television format of the twenty-first century. It fills television schedules around the globe, as well as thriving on streaming and video sharing platforms which host new programmes and provide access to vast archives of content. Its stories and personalities are not only found on television screens but also in online forums, social media, celebrity magazines and newspaper gossip columns.

Reality's techniques and tropes can be seen everywhere from 'mockumentary' comedies to found footage horror films; from sci-fi to soap opera. It has made new stars, revitalised the careers of failing celebrities and even seen one of its biggest characters ascend to the US Presidency.

Reality television has been praised for giving a platform to ordinary people, raising awareness of social issues and revitalising factual programming. Yet, it has been criticised by parents, politicians and pundits for sensationalism, manipulation and its potential to cause harm to its participants. So, what is it about it that makes it so fascinating? Why do we love it, hate it and, indeed, love to hate it?

In this book, I am going to get 'under the skin' of the phenomenon and to consider the current state of the genre as we enter the third decade of the twenty-first century.

CHAPTER STRUCTURE

Chapter 1 provides an overview of reality television, exploring what it is and where it comes from. It brings together key ideas from academics, participants, producers and journalists about the history and nature of reality television, outlines key programme formats and explores the various ways shows are, or are not, considered 'reality' by the TV industry, participants, audiences and commentators.

Chapter 2 moves on to consider the impact reality television has had on culture and the media, and explores the relationship the genre has with its audience. It looks at key debates in the study and analysis of reality TV, the impact of reality television on other forms of media, and the relationship between reality TV and its audiences.

Chapter 3 explores reality television as an industry. It looks at issues of ethics and duty of care, processes of regulation, production and distribution, the role of advertising and product placement, issues of labour, and supplementary industries and products.

Chapter 4 focuses more closely on what happens in reality television, exploring its characters, formats, messages and stories in more depth. The chapter considers the casting mix of different reality shows and looks at the reasons people take part in reality shows.

Chapter 5 discusses Reality TV (RTV)'s relationship to fame. It explores the way it has made stars of 'ordinary' people and considers why some of its key performers have managed to sustain long careers in the spotlight whilst others have disappeared. The chapter also explores the appeal of reality for 'traditional' celebrities and what it can do for their image.

Finally, Chapter 6 looks at the role of reality television in an age of social media. It discusses the different ways the genre has capitalised on the internet, discusses social media strategies for TV shows, considers what the role of reality television is in an age of YouTube and influencers, and, finally, offers some thoughts as to where the genre might be headed.

MY APPROACH

This book is intended as a quick guide to reality television as a phenomenon, taking in a range of factors affecting its production and content – from different viewpoints, including participants, regulators, producers and critics.

Throughout the book, there will be extracts from interviews I have conducted with participants and professionals from the UK and Ireland. In line with my university's ethics board recommendations, most have chosen to remain anonymous, including the name of the shows they participated in – some of these shows ran for a single episode or series; thus, naming them would expose the interviewees' identities. Others have been happy to name the programmes they have been involved in, and some have asked to be named specifically. Commentary taken from audience members in forums, blogs and social media has been anonymised to give some privacy towards the authors.

Given the number of reality shows now runs into the thousands, if not tens of thousands, I could use the entirety of this book just trying to list them all – and the same is, of course, true of the many books and articles written about the phenomenon. So, if I have missed out your favourite, please forgive me!

I have tried to use a range of international examples, but as an author based in the UK, there are inevitably more from the UK. Likewise, I have attempted to reference a range of international perspectives on the phenomenon, but I am aware that a lot of the scholarship on reality television has been concentrated in the UK, the USA and Australia; therefore, whilst there are certainly some global trends we can identify, I acknowledge that authors from elsewhere in the world might have a very different take on some key issues.

Much has been written about reality television over the years, and this is a small book! So, my approach is primarily to think about reality television as it stands as the twenty-first century enters its third decade – how has it developed, who its stars are, how it sits within a world of streaming and social media, and where might it be going in the future.

Finally, just a note about me – I am a media and communications scholar, and an entertainment critic. I have been watching reality TV shows since before we even called them that! The genre has educated, entertained and enraged me in fairly equal measures over the years, and I come to this as a critical friend, rather than someone who wants to tear the whole thing down. And to pre-empt the inevitable question, I doubt I would ever choose to go on one (although, obviously, I have chosen the songs I would use if I were ever on *Strictly Come Dancing*, and have thought long and hard about my *Big Brother* gameplay strategy) – but I salute all those brave souls who have!

1

UNDERSTANDING REALITY TV

Reality shows can be deeply serious or deliriously silly. They deal with the 'ordinary' and the 'extraordinary'. They have covered everything from colonialism to colonic irrigation and featured everyone from porn stars to priests. Interested in farming, tattoo artistry, pottery, Islamic dress, cocktail making or conducting an orchestra? Reality TV has got it covered. Do you want to get an insight into birth, death, marriage, divorce, friendship, work and community? The same applies.

Graeme Turner (2010) argues that it 'may well be the most exorbitantly "noticed" form of programming in television's history' (p. 33), and Jon Dovey (2000) calls it the 'perfect televisual form for the contemporary cultural moment ... [it has become] a crucial component of the fabric of popular culture' (p. 78).

Reality brings together techniques from documentary, game show, soap opera, melodrama and sitcom, yet is not readily classifiable as any of these things. So, what binds a diverse set of programmes and themes together and makes them 'reality'? And, where did these shows come from in the first place?

Unfortunately, these questions are not easy to answer! There is no clear consensus on either what reality television is, or where it comes from. Multiple programmes have been cited as 'the first' reality show, including *Candid Camera* (1947–2004) and its radio predecessor, *Candid Microphone* (1947), ...*Up* (1964–), *An American Family* (1973), *The Family* (1974), *Unsolved Mysteries* (1987–2010), *Cops* (1989–), *The Real World* (1992–), *Survivor* (1999–) and *Big Brother* (1999–) (for longer discussions on the history of the genre, see Bignell, 2005; Bonner, 2003; Dovey, 2000; Hill, 2005; Kavka, 2012).

In a way, it is not a surprise that all of these (and more) have been considered originators of the reality genre. They are all considered landmark television programmes that marked a watershed moment in TV production by offering something 'different'. All have served as pioneers in factual TV production, with many imitators coming in their wake. Whilst they used different filming, editing and narrative techniques – each was concerned in different ways with the 'ordinary', and aimed to unearth social and personal 'truths' in new ways.

Part of the reason that it is hard to establish a single text as the key point at which a phenomenon was born lies in the fact that it is hard to pin down exactly what we mean by 'reality television'. All of the shows listed above could be seen as reality television, as, in topic and format, they clearly resemble the kinds of programmes we identify today as belonging to the genre, including: a focus on the personal; 'ordinary' people and their experiences; highly constructed and formatted presentation; a blend of factual reportage with entertainment values such as humour and emotion (Dovey, 2000; Kavka, 2012). However, we could also argue that none, or at least very few, of these are technically reality TV – because when they were broadcast, the term had not been invented yet, and television schedules had yet to be saturated by this kind of programming.

Academic and journalistic accounts have included almost the full range of factual programming under the banner 'reality television', including genres we may not always see as 'obviously' fitting its remit, such as quiz shows, antiques programming, chat shows and nature programming. Indeed, news coverage is possibly the only factual genre to escape the term, and even that has been discussed in terms of its relationship with reality (Bennett, 2005; Hill, 2007).

WHERE DID 'REALITY TV' COME FROM ANYWAY?

The term 'reality television' became commonplace in different academic studies during the 1990s, with early literature focussing on crime, consumer affairs and disaster formats (e.g. *999, Cops, Crimewatch*). The makeover, talk show and 'docusoap' formats of the 1990s (e.g. *Changing Rooms, Jerry Springer, Airport*) meant that the focus of the literature and the use of the term 'reality television' expanded to include these genres. 'Social experiments' (e.g. *The 1900 House, Survivor, Big Brother*), which emerged at the turn of the millennium, expanded the genre further, as did the early 00s' resurgence in talent shows heralded by the *Popstars* and *Pop Idol* franchises – to the point where reality has moved away from being a single genre, and, instead becomes more of what Nick Couldry (2009) terms a 'meta-genre' (p. 47) encompassing several subgenres.

It is hard to pinpoint the first use of the phrase within the TV industry, or in journalistic and academic accounts of the phenomenon. Academic studies have certainly been using the term since at least the 1990s (e.g. Dauncey, 1996; Kilborn & Izod, 1997); however, it is harder to trace its origins in industry or popular discourse. For example, searching for the term in English language news database Nexis returns very few articles using the term 'reality television' before the late 1990s, and a modest number between 1997 and 1999 – and the returned results do not always use the term to indicate a genre, more to describe the ethos of an individual show. In contrast, when searching in 2000–2001, Nexis returns thousands of hits, as the arrival of popular global formats such as the *Idol* franchises, *Big Brother* and *Survivor* saw the term 'reality television' become a common component of media culture.

The way academics, audiences and the industry use the term 'reality TV' also fluctuates over time. Dovey (2000), for example, considers British crime show *Crimewatch* (a studio-based show involving crime reconstructions and public appeals) to be reality television; whereas now, it would be considered unusual by broadcasters and audiences to think of *Crimewatch* as a reality show when compared to an observational programme dealing with crime such as *24 hours in Police Custody*, which more closely fits the template of what we consider reality television in terms of its use of on-the-spot filming, strong characters, social commentary, voice-over narration and story-like narratives.

DEFINING REALITY TV

Most academic studies, rather than attempting to pin down a definition of reality TV, highlight that it is almost impossible to coming up with strict rules as to what it is and is not:

> *to narrow the definition [of RTV] is not necessarily helpful; it obscures the flexibility inherent to 'reality TV'. (Couldry, 2003, p. 10)*

However, even if it is difficult to completely pin down a definition, there are some features that seem to be common to reality programming. Dover and Hill (2007, p. 25) argue that it usually features a combination of information, education and entertainment; and Hill (2005) also points out that it 'implicitly and explicitly addresses the viewers about good and bad ways to live their lives' (p. 184) whilst Corner (2004) says it is about 'ordinary people doing ordinary things' (p. 295).

At the heart of all 'reality' TV, however, is some sort of claim to the 'real'. However, the term 'real' can sometimes seem to be the antithesis of what is actually involved in reality TV – when I mention to people that I am researching the field, the most common response I get is along the lines of 'well, they're all fake, anyway'. I will look at issues of 'real' versus 'fake' in more detail in later chapters, but at the heart of this tension is that 'real' can be interpreted in many ways.

Naturally, the confines of a TV time slot mean that showing unvarnished reality 'as it happens' is impossible – there has to be a process of selection and editing (not least as unvarnished reality contains a lot of mundane activity that does not make for good television!). Reality shows vary in what they mean by the 'real' – there are observational and hidden camera formats that attempt to show people 'naturally' going about their daily lives, for example, but there are also shows that place people in contrived situations that may be very different from their ordinary life. In historical reality TV like *The 1900 Island* or *Back in Time For...*, the idea is for contemporary participants to experience something of the reality of their historical peers. In a format like *I'm a Celebrity: Get Me Out of Here!* however, the focus is on the 'real' people behind the celebrity façade – they do not 'really' live in the jungle and eat bugs, but the show uses these testing situations to reveal their emotions, personalities, make-up free faces and other aspects of the 'real' person. As Turner (2010) explains:

> *The formats usually included under this label have a quite varied relation to 'the real': some are highly narrativized and mediated, some are actually just updated game shows for whom the 'reality' descriptor is more an indicator of format style than any claim to be capturing real life, and still others are essentially documentary in their format and in their ethical relation to the material they put before viewers. (p. 33)*

According to Bignell (2005), one of the chief points of reality TV is:

> *For people to reveal themselves to each other and to the audience, to establish a 'structure of feeling' that the television audience can share and adduce to understand the foibles, embarrassments and triumphs of the participants, who are most often presented as familiar and ordinary. (p. 172–173)*

June Deery (2015) argues that what many reality shows deal in is 'staged actuality' – by which she means they contain a mixture of contrived and spontaneous situations (p. 29).

If the term has many uses, then, and these not only shift according to time but also according to context and, even, to the individual using it, is the term reality television still fit for purpose? I would argue that it is, insofar as it still has resonance and meaning in different contexts. There are perceptions of what reality television is, even though they differ. It is seen as something that has value for audiences and participants as much as it is also seen as an object of derision and low culture elsewhere. And if we were to abandon the term altogether, how then would we categorise some of the shows that typically come under its banner, and examine what we might learn from thinking about them in connection with one another?

I would argue that 'reality television' has about as much, and as little, usefulness as comparative genre terms like 'documentary' or 'game show'. There are almost infinite permutations of what each term means, yet they still echo something that connects with audiences, in however limited capacity. For the purposes of this book, I am taking a broad approach to the term. Rather than trying to narrow down its definition to a select group of programmes, I would prefer we open up the definition and consider the breadth of content that it can encompass. Therefore, I am including any television programme that has, at its heart, an emphasis on the 'real' lived and or felt experiences of people – be they ordinary citizens, celebrities or even elites.

I have kept a deliberately broad definition to recognise the diversity of the format, and acknowledge how blurred the lines are between 'reality' and 'documentary', 'game show' or 'entertainment'. For example, *The Only Way Is Essex*, which is a non-competitive show (unless we are talking about the competition for airtime and attention) has, perhaps, more in common with a so-called observational documentary such as *63Up* than it does with a skill-based competition such as *MasterChef*.

I am not arguing against using other terms like documentary or game show to describe programmes – on the contrary, I believe that in many cases, more than one genre classification is not only helpful but also necessary. I consider it perfectly possible that something could be a documentary and a reality show at the same time, for example. I am also concerned with challenging the discourse found particularly within the world of programme makers and broadcasters, that implies that documentary as a genre is more 'serious' than RTV, has something more 'substantial' to say, or has in any way a greater claim to 'truth' – after all, documentaries involve the same processes of selecting, editing and framing their material.

That said, there are some programmes that I am excluding from my discussion – even though others may decide to include them in their own analyses. I will be focussing on programmes that deal with humans, rather than animals. There are certainly some nature programmes that take a similar approach to human-focussed reality shows (eg *Meerkat Manor, Orangutan Island*), and try to anthropomorphise them by attributing human emotions to them. However, as we cannot ever 'know' the inner thoughts and feelings of the animal kingdom in the same way we can with humans; they are perhaps too different to be considered alongside other reality shows.

I have also excluded documentaries where the principal objective is some form of investigation of a particular issue or theme; for example, documentaries investigating climate change or anti-terror legislation. Whilst there may be a human interest and reality component to them, this is not the core focus of the documentary. I am also excluding magazine-style shows because their format is comprised of several small segments rather than detailed stories. Likewise, chat shows are excluded as being a primarily promotional vehicle for the celebrities involved and centred on the personalities of the hosts. Game shows and quiz shows are, for the most part, also left out of this book – although there are some exceptions, for example, *Survivor* or *Big Brother* where there is a game element to the programme; but this is, perhaps, secondary to the experience and personalities of those involved.

WHAT DOES REALITY TV LOOK LIKE?

Not only is it difficult for writers to establish a consensus on what 'reality' television is, but also it is a term that remains equally evasive for production companies and broadcasters. Indeed, the same programme may be referred to differently by viewers, broadcasters, journalists, participants, makers and media companies. Even companies making these shows often assign multiple genre categories to the same shows when they are marketing them, in order to maximise potential reach.

There is also potentially some snobbery at work on behalf of the industry in the way that some broadcasters want to avoid using the term 'reality' altogether. The genre has a history of being maligned which I will discuss later in the book, and carries with it some undesirable connotations (Dovey, 2000; Hill, 2019).

In the British context, for example, none of the streaming services for the major broadcasters (BBC iPlayer, ITV Hub, All 4, My5) have 'reality' as a category at all, preferring 'factual', 'lifestyle', 'documentary' and 'entertainment'. This may, in part, be connected to these broadcasters all having public service remits, and reality being perceived as less 'serious' or 'educational' than some other factual formats – although it is probably also in part due to the difficulties associated with defining reality.

Even some production companies shy away from the term: World of Wonder (makers of *RuPaul's Drag Race, Dancing Queen* and more) mention 'entertaining hit series' and 'documentaries' on their website; Love Productions (home of the *The Great British Bake Off, Benefits Street* and dozens of other reality-style shows) prefer 'ground breaking hit formats', 'agenda-setting documentaries' and 'popular singles and series'; KEO Films (*Eden, Too Fat For Love* etc) simply label their shows 'ratings powerhouses and awards winners'. These three are not isolated cases – and even in the case of production companies and broadcasters that do use the term 'reality', it is interesting which programmes do and do not make the cut – there is a tendency that, the more serious the topic of the programme, the less likely it is to be labelled 'reality'. Conversely, on Netflix, which has an interface arguably more tailored to viewers than the wider industry (and which does not have the public service commitments of many national broadcasters), the reality categories contain a broad spectrum of factual programming.

The difficulty of categorising factual programmes extends to other aspects of the media industry, such as the awards ceremonies held around the world to celebrate TV achievements. Ceremonies differ greatly when it comes to the number of categories they use for factual programmes, and in how shows are assigned.

For example, the British Academy of Film and Television Awards (BAFTAs) include a range of categories of factual media, all of which include programmes that elsewhere might be categorised as reality television (Fig. 1).

Fig. 1. BAFTA Nominees 2019.

Category	Nominees
Features	*Who Do You Think You Are?, The Great British Bake Off, Mortimer and Whitehouse Gone Fishing, Gordon, Gino and Fred's Road Trip*
Specialist factual	*Suffragettes with Lucy Worsley, Grayson Perry's Rites of Passage, Superkids: Breaking Away From Care, Bros: After the Screaming*
Entertainment	*Britain's Got Talent, Strictly Come Dancing, Ant and Dec's Saturday Night Takeaway, Michael McIntyre's Big Show*
Factual series	*Louis Theroux's Altered States, Prison, 24 Hours in A&E, Life and Death Row: The Mass Execution*
Reality and constructed factual	*I'm a Celebrity … Get Me Out of Here!, Old People's Home for 4 Year-Olds, The Real Full Monty, Dragon's Den*
Single documentary	*Gun No. 6, My Dad, The Peace Deal and Me, Driven: The Billy Monger Story, School for Stammers*
Current affairs	*Myanmar's Killing Fields, Exposure, The Ballymurphy Precedent, Football's Wall of Silence*

It is not readily apparent what the distinctions between these categories are. What makes *The Great British Bake Off (GBBO)* a 'Feature', when *Strictly Come Dancing* is 'Entertainment'? Both, after all, both focus on people learning a specialist skill and being voted off each week. Why is *Bros: After the Screaming Stops* a 'specialist factual' and *Driven: The Billy Monger Story* a 'single documentary'? Both are one-off features utilising observational and interview techniques and both explore what happens once success has dissipated. Indeed, we could critique the whole list in this way and argue that the categories primarily serve to give a wider range of programmes a chance to win.

To extend this example, let us take a look at the way other ceremonies in the UK, the USA and Australia (Figs. 2–4) deal with categorisation.

Fig. 2. Emmy Nominees 2018 (USA).

Category	Nominees
Structured reality	*Who Do You Think You Are?, Antiques Roadshow, Fixer Upper, Lip Sync Battle, Queer Eye, Shark Tank*
Unstructured reality	*Born This Way, Deadliest Catch, Intervention, Naked and Afraid, RuPaul's Drag Race: Untucked, United States of America with Kamau Bell*
Competition program	*American Ninja Warrior, Project Runway, RuPaul's Drag Race, The Amazing Race, The Voice, Top Chef*
Documentary or non-fiction series	*American Masters, Blue Planet II, The Defiant Ones, The Fourth Estate, Wild Wild Country*
Directory or non-fiction special	*Icarus, Jim and Andy: The Great Beyond, Mister Rogers: Its You I Like, Spielberg, The Zen Diaries of Garry Shandling*
International series or special	*Antony Bourdain: Parts Unknown, Leah Remini: Scientology and the Aftermath, My Next Guest Needs No Introduction, Star Talk, Vice*

Fig. 3. Logies 2018 (Australia).

Category	Nominees
Entertainment	*Gogglebox Australia, Anh's Brush With Fame, Family Feud, Hard Quiz, The Project*
Reality	*The Block, I'm a Celebrity… Get Me Out of Here!, Married at First Sight, My Kitchen Rules, Travel Guides*
Lifestyle	*The Living Room, Better Homes and Gardens, Gardening Australia, Selling Houses Australia, The Checkout*
Documentary	*War on Waste, Michael Hutchence: The Last Rockstar, Struggle Street, The Queen and Zack Grieve, You Can't Ask That*

Fig. 4. National Television Awards (NTAs) 2019 (UK).

Category name	Nominees
Talent show	*All Together Now, Britain's Got Talent, Dancing on Ice, Strictly Come Dancing, The Voice UK, The Voice Kids, The X Factor*
Factual entertainment	*All or Nothing: Manchester City, Ambulance, Animals with Cameras, Antiques Roadshow, Attenborough and the Giant Elephant, Big Cats, Countryfile, Cruising with Jane McDonald, Digging for Britain, DIY SOS, Fake or Fortune?, Gogglebox, Heathrow: Britain's Busiest Airport, MasterChef, Match of the Day, Michael Palin in North Korea, Misfits Like Us, Paul O'Grady: For the Love of Dogs, Queer Eye, Reported Missing, The Apprentice, The Grand Tour, The Great British Bake Off, The One Show, The Real Full Monty, The Real Marigold Hotel, The Truth About …, Tom Kerridge's Lose Weight For Good, Who Do You Think You Are?*
Entertainment	*All Round to Mrs Brown's, And They're Off, Ant and Dec's Saturday Night Takeaway, Big Star's Little Star, Blind Date, Celebrity Juice, Harry Hill's Alien Fun Capsule, Have I Got News For You, I'm a Celebrity … Get Me Out Of Here!, Love Island, Michael McIntyre's Big Show, Mock the Week, My Next Guest Needs No Introduction, Ninja Warrior UK, Piers Morgan's Life Stories, Take Me Out, The Big Narstie Show, The Graham Norton Show, The Jonathan Ross Show, The Last Leg, The Luke McQueen Pilots. This Time Next Year, Through the Keyhole, Would I Lie To You?, You've Been Framed*

Looking at these lists is both exhausting and confusing! Programmes might appear in multiple categories, or in categories that sometimes make little sense. What these lists do show us, however, is that, whilst there are dozens of different types of factual and reality shows, we might, at least, be able to attempt to loosely group them into a few key categories, whether by theme (e.g. dating, cookery), or by format.

As there are so many potential themes, perhaps it might be easier to consider the differences in format instead. The following list covers the broad spectrum of common reality formats – although lots of shows are a hybrid of several of these formats and also include elements of other genres, such as comedy and soap opera.

Talent and Skill

These are probably one of the earliest examples of what we have come to call reality TV – think of twentieth century formats like *Junior Showtime, New Faces* or *Young Talent Time*. Some shows deal with novices learning together, others deal with professionals or highly skilled amateurs competing at an advanced level. The format involves several competitors who give performances, or complete tasks and challenges. Their success is usually judged by an expert panel, a public vote or both, until one competitor is left victorious.

Examples include: *American Idol, Got Talent, MasterChef, Dancing With the Stars* and *I Am Singer*

Observational/Fly-on-the-Wall

These shows are filmed as if we are a fly on the wall, watching the action that unfolds around us. At the heart of the genre is the idea that we are merely observers of naturally occurring interactions (Kilborn & Izod, 1997). Even if that is an illusion, and scenes are set up, rehearsed and re-shot (as is the case in most shows), the idea is that we should feel as though we are observing something organic and natural. Most observational shows employ some form of voice-over commentary to frame the action, and this can be serious, or, especially in the case of the 'docusoap' format, humorous (see Chapter 3). Observational shows do not usually involve some kind of competition or prize, although observational techniques are used in some competitive shows, such as *Big Brother*, which blends aspects of several of the subgenres listed here.

Examples include: *Airport, Sylvania Waters* and *The Mighty Redcar.*

Hidden Camera

These shows share some characteristics with observational formats, in that the viewer is watching things occur 'naturally'. However, whereas people in observational shows usually know they are being filmed, the subjects of hidden camera shows are often unaware. This format is usually used to highlight 'bad' behaviour, whether that is criminal activity, poor professional practice or something more benign, like cheating on a diet. The person(s) caught on hidden camera are then usually shown their bad behaviour and punished, or encouraged to repent. Often, more hidden cameras will then be used to track whether or not the person has really changed their habits.

Examples include: *Kitchen Nightmares, The Hotel Inspector* and *Traffic Cops.*

Makeover

This type of show focuses on someone, something or somewhere, being 'made over' or transformed in some capacity.

The transformation is often seen as a symbol of personal growth or change, and this, rather than a trophy or cash prize, is seen as the reward for participation. Most of these shows feature a regular cast of experts involved in the makeover, with new subjects in each episode.

Examples include: *Queer Eye, What Not to Wear* and *Tidying Up With Marie Kondo*.

Video Diaries

This format involves an individual (or individuals) filming their own life and experiences, generally with the role of any camera crew minimised. The video diary format typically involves moments of confessional, where the subject directly addresses the camera to reveal some particular 'truth'. Even in formats that utilise other approaches, there are often moments of video diary confessional included, where participants share their thoughts away from the wider group. Video diaries can also be seen as a clear precursor for vlogs, which we will look at more in Chapter 6.

Examples include: *Video Nation, Video Diaries* and *60 Days on the Streets*.

Social or Lifestyle Experiment

In many ways a hybrid of the observational, makeover and video diary formats, the experiment show involves an individual or group experiencing a new routine or way of life for a fixed period of time. This will often involve participants travelling to a new environment, living by a set of rules, facing difficulty in letting go of old habits and ending up having learned something about themselves or others. This genre is often combined with more traditional factual TV formats, such as travel or history programming and promoted as 'educational' in focus.

Examples include: *Wife Swap, The 1900 House* and *Married at First Sight.*

Scripted Reality

This is a genre that blossomed in the mid-2000s with shows like *The Hills* and *The Only Way is Essex*. Essentially, it takes the established fly-on-the-wall format of watching people in their ordinary lives, especially following the template of the 'docusoap' format, where small communities of people make up the cast. However, instead of presenting the action as simply unfolding before our eyes naturally, several situations are deliberately contrived/scripted for these shows to amplify the emotional response of participants – and the programmes are completely open about this aspect. These scenarios have a basis in, and are sometimes an exaggeration of, existing experiences in the participants' lives. The result is a mixture of genuine lived experiences coupled with scenarios completely fabricated for the programme, and hence their presentation as scripted 'reality' rather than pure fiction.

Examples include: *The Hills, Jersey Shore* and *Made in Chelsea.*

Studio Discussion

Studio-based discussion in front of a live audience forms the heart of talk shows like *Jerry Springer and Jeremy Kyle*. Studio discussion is also most commonly the style adopted in reality spin-off shows, which often include a panel of experts, celebrities or former contestants commenting on what has just been shown. Whilst these are most commonly separate entities from the 'main' show (and may even be online-only or shown on a different channel), some reality shows, such as *Terrace House* or *Sex Box*, embed studio discussion into the main programme format. Others, like most versions of *Big Brother*, use studio interviews with the evicted contestant and the host as a weekly ritual.

Examples include: *Big Brother's Bit on the Side, The Great British Bake Off: An Extra Slice* and *The Jeremy Kyle Show.*

Other Specialist Factual

There are a few other forms of factual programming that are sometimes included in academic and industry discussions of reality television, but which do not readily align with the categories listed above. This may include specialist genres such as sports, art, music, nature, motoring, consumer affairs, quiz shows, variety and true crime. We might also include magazine shows that mix reality-style features with reviews, current affairs and celebrity interviews.

Then there are special interest shows that contain some reality components and are sometimes discussed as 'reality' but do not easily fit into the more common categories listed above. For example, *Antiques Roadshow* features 'ordinary' people getting possessions appraised by experts, and the show often includes vignettes about the stories behind the object. There are 'reveal' moments when the value is given, and emotional reactions. However, the show is ultimately focused more on the items than the individuals.

Examples include: *Songs of Praise, Top Gear* and *Making a Murderer.*

CONCLUSION

Reality TV is a complex beast – it contains so many permutations that it is hard to define. It encompasses a whole range of themes and formats, and whilst it is all concerned with 'the real', what 'the real' means is different in almost every programme. But, what can we learn from considering the phenomenon as a whole? In the rest of this book, I will explore some of the key themes and debates that academics, industry professionals, audiences and reality participants themselves grapple with.

2

HOW REALITY TV CHANGED THE WORLD

One of the defining events of the 2010s was Donald Trump's election to President of the USA in 2016. A media storm was created during his campaigning that has yet to die down (at the time of writing). A gregarious and divisive figure, Trump and his rise to power has been endlessly analysed and critiqued by journalists, academics, fellow politicians and members of the public-not only in America but also worldwide.

One of the key themes in this discussion is the role reality television has played in the ascent of Trump. In 2004, the businessman was chosen as the face of reality show *The Apprentice*, a role he played for 14 seasons (plus celebrity editions) until politics came calling. The grand stage of a reality competition that thrives on grand gestures of charisma and power enabled him to become adept at drawing attention to the point where:

> *As Trump regularly proclaims and the media slavishly illustrate, he is 'ratings gold', the king of 'earned' media. (Hearn, 2016, p. 656)*

Having spent over a decade honing his public image through this programme (and associated media like autobiographies and self-aggrandising interviews), Trump was able to create and stage his image to give the impression he was a successful businessman (even if some of the records of his business affairs throw doubt on this claim), shrewd judge of character and talent, and a confident leader, traits that translate well into the political arena:

> *The presentation of Trump in TA/CA was decidedly*
> *presidential – he alone made the decisions about*
> *who would stay or go, his decisions were always*
> *right within the narrative of the show, and he*
> *was able to make the decision fairly and quickly*
> *(Gabriel et al., 2015, p. 305).*

Whilst Gabriel et al. suggest that this reality-crafted image may have been a factor in boosting his public support, it also became a source of contention for his critics. Laurie Oullette (2016) notes that many commentators bemoaned the arrival of

> *unseemly reality TV theatrics into electoral politics.*
> *'A couple of years ago Donald Trump was just*
> *a barker on a carnival show, now he's as good a*
> *bet for president, with Dog the Bounty Hunter or*
> *Octomom for his vice president', professed Rex*
> *Murphy (2016) of the Canadian Broadcasting*
> *Corporation in a television editorial that went viral.*
> *'You want to pretend life is a TV show? Well now*
> *you have your wish', he smugly told the camera,*
> *blaming not just the TV industry, but masses of*
> *indiscriminating reality TV viewers for Trump's*
> *political ascendancy. (p. 647)*

Trump presents an extreme example of the (perceived) impact of reality television on global politics and culture – and it should be noted that reality TV is just one of many possible factors contributing to his success – but, it highlights a range of the key debates about the role of reality television in public life, including its relationship with politics and governance, its influence on its audience, and its power to create celebrity, as well as the complex interplay between the 'real' and the staged, the ordinary and the theatrical.

In this chapter, I will explore the importance of reality television in more detail, focussing on three key areas: themes in the study of reality TV, its impact on wider media and its relationship to its audience.

REALITY TV'S BIG IDEAS

Reality television has been repeatedly scrutinised from every angle by all kinds of interested parties, including politicians, business leaders, academics, journalists, regulators, producers, audiences and participants. Even though the body of analysis of RTV is vast, there are a few themes that recur.

One of the most important is the idea of citizenship. Reality trades in ideas about what it means to be a good citizen, at both the individual level and the level of community. One central idea is that reality television helps promote values associated with *neo-liberalism*, a system of values that privileges good citizenship as being about enterprise. In neo-liberal politics, the responsibility of the state to care for the welfare of its citizens is sidestepped, 'with the responsibility for dealing with the complexities of everyday life increasingly lying with the "enterprising" self and the privatized, "informed" citizen' (Lewis, 2007, p. 286).

In the neo-liberal world, the individual is considered responsible for self-improvement and contribution to society, and must put in 'hard work', both in the fields of employment and personal life, in order to receive the benefits of material goods and an improved lot in life. One key mechanism for this self-improvement comes in the form of the 'makeover' and the promise that material goods, self-help and other techniques of self-improvement can make one a better citizen:

> *Makeovers justify their activities by claiming transformation enhances self-esteem, which, in turn, allows for a form of personal empowerment but also for citizenship status. By rectifying the distance between social ideals and lived experience, makeovers propose to make lives happier and participants more powerful. (Weber, 2009, pp. 255–256)*

Whilst makeover culture can be found in a whole range of cultural and social phenomena, it is central to reality television (Redden, 2007; Ringrose & Walkerdine, 2008) as individuals submit themselves to a process of reinvention in order to become better versions of themselves and function more effectively within the social sphere (we will explore how this works in practice in Chapter 4).

It is worth pointing out here that neo-liberalism is key to many Western societies, but this is not necessarily a global perspective – in many Arab countries, for example, they are heavily critical of the neo-liberal ideas in Western formats, seeing these as not representing the 'reality' of the Arab way of life (Kraidy, 2011).

Key to the process of ensuring good citizenship is the role of *surveillance*. This refers to the idea that we are, at all times, under scrutiny from authorities and our fellow citizens – that is, we are always both watching others and being watched;

that 'watching' is rarely neutral but involves judgements on behaviour, taste and respectability. As Michel Foucault (1977) puts it, 'the judges of normality are everywhere' (p. 304). A common metaphor used to describe this process is the 'panopticon' – a structure with many sides from which everything around it can be observed (Dover & Hill, 2007; Foucault, 1977).

Reality TV functions as one form of surveillance, or what Skeggs and Wood (2012) term, a 'technology of governmentality' (p. 4). It is just one example (the internet, CCTV and mobile phones are others) of a growing social anxiety about the pervasiveness and normalisation of surveillance techniques in everyday life. In RTV, individuals are observed by hidden cameras, mentors and judges, each other, and, ultimately, the audience. Reality TV makes clear what is wrong with people, what needs to be changed, which kinds of behaviour should be rewarded and which punished.

One key way in which reality television creates ideas about good citizenship is through its depiction of 'community'. This community can operate on a geographical level (think about the way talent shows ask us to vote for contestants from our home city or region to demonstrate they 'belong' to us), a national level, a pan-national level (i.e. belonging to a region such as Africa or the Arab world), an identity level (e.g. the idea that an individual might represent the disabled or LGBTQ+communities) or a more general level (i.e. how people live and operate together).

However, to be a good citizen usually means engaging with that community in some level. For example, in *The Secret Millionaire*, volunteers and charity workers perform good citizenship – but so do the millionaire benefactors bestowing surprise wealth upon them (Biressi, 2011), whilst in *Big Brother*, good citizenship is about how one behaves in relation to the other housemates: voting fairly, performing tasks to benefit the house, not eating more than one's share of food, not 'backstabbing', etc.

Some of these ideas about community and citizenship are inscribed explicitly into formats – for example, in many British makeover and lifestyle experiments, 'the "problems" of the participants are conflated with the "problems" of contemporary Britain' (Deller, 2014, p. 296) and it is implied that the impact of the makeover will have wider social ramifications:

> *Britain is in a mess. Anti-social behaviour [shots of*
> *people drinking], binge drinking and promiscuity*
> *are rife .... Imam Ajmal Masroor wants Britain*
> *to rediscover the values of decency, respect and*
> *moderation.... Can a 1400-year-old religion really*
> *sort out these people's lives? (Make Me a Muslim,*
> S1 E1)

The idea of community is not always straightforward. For example, there have been pan-African and pan-Arab versions of *Big Brother*, and pan-Arab talent shows like *Star Academy* and *Superstar*. Whilst these programmes aimed to promote the virtues of regional togetherness (as well as being more cost-effective than each nation producing its own editions), in practice there were several problems as the political climate, and ideas of 'morality' varied from nation to nation, leading to bans, restrictions and political argument in places like Saudi Arabia and Kuwait (Ghattas, 2012; Jacobs, 2007; Kraidy, 2011, 2014).

DIVERSITY IN REALITY TV

One way that reality television demonstrates its commitment to showing ideal community and good citizenship is through its relationship to diversity. It is one of, if not *the*, the most diverse broadcasting genres, not only in the scope of topics it covers but also in the range of participants featured. It has been a core site of representation for members of minority ethnic, religious, disabled and LGBTQ + communities as well as for members of niche interest groups, employees of a wide range of industries and people of different ages, class groups, and nationalities (Gamson, 2014; Kraidy & Sender, 2012; Lovelock, 2016; Lovelock, 2019; Stephens, 2004).

There are several reasons why this might be. Firstly, reality shows tend to feature large casts, meaning there is more scope for featuring a diverse range of participants. Secondly, they are able to recruit relatively easily through social media, connections with affinity and community groups and public calls for participants – and reality TV has a low entry bar in that participants do not need an agent or any specific training (unlike, say, actors). Thirdly, the stories that are told by RTV do not necessarily need the same amount of research as a drama or investigative documentary, as participants also bring their own experiences and stories to the table, making it much easier to slot in people from a variety of backgrounds.

In some countries, broadcasters are expected to abide by particular policies and guidelines regarding representation, from issues of 'fairness' to having quotas to meet in terms of staffing and representation. This is particularly the case for broadcasters with a public service remit. Reality television presents an easy way for broadcasters to demonstrate their commitment to meeting diversity targets and presenting themselves as inclusive.

For example, in the most recent annual report from UK broadcaster Channel 4, 22 reality and documentary programmes are singled out as helping the channel meet diversity requirements compared to six shows from other genres (Channel 4, 2018, comedy, drama, quiz shows, news and sport).

However, whilst there are clearly many positive aspects to featuring people from diverse backgrounds, the history of representation in reality television is problematic, to put it mildly! There have been accusations of reality TV trading in crude stereotypes such as the overly camp gay man (Deller, 2012b; Lovelock, 2016); the taste-free 'chav' (Tyler & Bennett, 2010); the 'workshy benefits scrounger' (Jensen, 2014; Tyler, 2013) or the 'angry black woman' (Bell-Jordan, 2008; Squires, 2014).

Reality TV has been criticised for 'enfreakment' of some participants through emphasising their difference from the 'norm' (Cleary, 2016; Friedman, 2014; Richardson, 2017; Smith, 2017). This can involve turning them into extreme caricatures such as *X Factor* UK reject 'The Chicken Man' (a man who worked in a chicken factory and could not sing, but may have had some mild learning difficulties), or it can occur in more subtle ways – for example, in Australia's *Instant Hotel*, all participants were described in terms of their relationship to each other (married couple; mother and daughter, etc.), but the lone gay male couple were the 'fussy couple'.

TV's narratives of good citizenship extend to telling people the correct way to 'perform' in relation to identity, from programmes like *Supersize vs Superskinny* or *Secret Eaters* that police people's weight and dietary habits, to the likes of *Snog, Marry, Avoid* and *How to Look Good Naked* that prescribe particular ways to perform gender through emphasising 'natural' beauty and modest-but-chic clothing. Whilst these interventions do apparently have benefits for the recipients (or so the TV narrative tells us), they offer a limited range of options of what is acceptable in terms of style, body shape, habit or appearance.

One of the most influential thinkers in this area is Pierre Bourdieu, and particularly his book *Distinction*

(1984). In this book, Bourdieu explains that 'capital' is crucial to one's success in society, but that material capital (money, property, possessions) is not the only important form of capital – social capital (connections) and cultural capital (our relationship to cultural items) are equally important. Whilst reality television focuses on all three of these, it is *cultural capital* that is often central. Certain forms of culture are seen as 'good' and others 'bad' – often expressed through the metaphor of 'taste'. Things that are in 'good taste' are often highly classed, racialised and gendered. Therefore, the styles of clothing, make-up, body and home valued in TV makeovers are not neutral examples of 'good taste' but represent particular values and sensibilities. In the case of Western TV, these things are often dictated by white, middle-class ideals, for example (Skeggs & Wood, 2012; Taylor, 2016; Wood & Skeggs, 2011).

Those that fit outside the boundaries of these values are either forced to change something about themselves to conform, or are cast in the role of what Imogen Tyler (2013) calls 'national abjects':

> *those groups within the population, such as the unemployed, welfare recipients and irregular migrants, who are imagined to be a parasitical drain and threat to national resources (p. 9).*

One heavily criticised form of reality television that deals in making these 'national abjects' is the 'Poverty porn' genre – shows like *Struggle Street* or *Benefits Street* that take what appears to be a fly-on-the-wall approach to benefits claimants but have been accused of framing the claimants as fraudulent and undeserving of welfare – in other words, bad citizens (Jensen, 2014; Runswick-Cole & Goodley, 2015).

In later chapters, we will see how some of these ideas play out in different reality shows.

HOW REALITY TELEVISION CHANGED
PRINT AND GOSSIP MEDIA

Reality shows do not exist in a vacuum, but in relation to one another, and to the wider media and entertainment industries. Therefore, to fully understand the impact of this phenomenon, it is worth considering the influence reality television has had on these industries.

The faces of reality personalities fill the pages of gossip sites, newspapers and magazines. As I write, the current cover of *OK!* magazine features a recent *Love Island* evictee and promises a confessional interview with her inside.[1] *Heat* magazine's cover features speculation on whether another *Love Islander* will win, teases a revealing interview with perpetual reality celeb, Kerry Katona, and revels in the break-up of reality presenter, Ant McPartlin, and his ex-wife, Lisa, the make-up artist on *Strictly Come Dancing*.[2] Newspaper the *Daily Star* has reality television stories as its front page headlines almost every day, and 50% of the *Daily Mail* website's 'sidebar of shame' (the right-hand sidebar that covers celebrity stories) focuses on reality stars.

In 2000, UK entertainment magazine *Heat* included *Big Brother* UK evictee, Andy Davidson, on its cover. It was something of an experiment for the publication, which, at the time, had a strong focus on television and film, rather than celebrity gossip. The issue was such a success that the magazine increased its coverage of the show – and the impact *Big Brother* had on the magazine was a core factor in it shifting its emphasis towards celebrity gossip (Kaur, 2007; Ritchie, 2000). It is not an isolated example – as many writers note, reality stars became staples of popular media. The vast number of them and their rapid turnover means they are a ready source of celebrity news and gossip – and their reality origins mean they are often skilled in techniques of personal revelation and confession, and in providing accounts of what 'really' happened on shows, what they are 'really' like and 'what happened next'. The presence of reality stars in print and online media serves multiple functions as well as providing content. They drive reality audiences to those outlets to continue the stories, alert readers to these shows, and they are also used in adverts and promotional campaigns for consumer goods that are featured online and in print publications (Cashmore, 2014; Kaur, 2007; Turner, 2014).

HOW REALITY TV CHANGED FICTIONAL MEDIA

Whilst reality television can be said to borrow techniques from fictional formats such as soap opera, comedy and drama, fictional formats, too, have repeatedly drawn upon the codes and conventions of reality television. Perhaps befitting reality's status as a genre that is portrayed as lightweight at best, and dangerous at worst, most fictionalised reality shows are satirical in nature, exaggerating the genre's worst excesses. Fictional reality TV is often shown collapsing in on itself, either through cancellation and tragedy, or through participants taking control of their own lives and leaving.

Craig Hight (2004) has argued that, broadly speaking, 'cinema's representation of television has tended to be a negative one' (p. 235). He notes that cinema often perceives the small screen to be a rival for viewers' attentions, and this sense of rivalry might partly explain the cynicism towards reality television found in films like *EdTV* (dir. Ron Howard, 1999) and *The Truman Show* (dir. Peter Weir, 1998). These two films, released during the docusoap boom but before the arrival of mega-reality brands like *Survivor* and *Big Brother*, follow an individual whose whole life is filmed 24/7 for TV and focus largely on the negative consequences of this constant surveillance, not only on Ed and Truman but also their friends and family, the viewers and culture as a whole. (There is also some amusement to be gained from seeing future reality judges Ellen DeGeneres and RuPaul sending up a genre that they would later be part of in *EdTV!*).

Hight also discusses *Series 7: The Contenders* (dir. Daniel Minahan, 2001), which sees reality show contestants fighting to kill each other, an idea replicated in several fictional media, including Ben Elton's novel *Dead Famous* (2001), the *Hunger Games* novels and film series (Collins, 2008–10; dirs. Gary Ross & Francis Lawrence, 2012–15) and horror flicks like *My Little Eye* (dir. Marc Evans, 2002). Indeed, horror as a genre has adopted several reality television techniques, including the rise of camcorder culture portrayed in 'found footage' films like *Cloverfield* (dir. Matt Reeves, 2008), *The Blair Witch Project* (dirs. Daniel Myrick & Eduardo Sánchez, 1999) and *Paranormal Activity* (dir. Oren Peli, 2007).

It is also probably no accident that the trend in cinema towards satirising reality television has, in more recent years, transferred to that other competitor for audience eyeballs, the internet, in films like *Unfriended* (dir. Levan Gabradze, 2014), *Friend Request* (dir. Simon Verhoeven, 2016) and *Men, Women and Children* (dir. Jason Reitman, 2014).

The satirisation of reality TV is not confined to cinema. Television comedy is rife with take-offs of the genre, from sketch shows (e.g. *Little Britain, Horrible Histories, Saturday Night Live*) to 'mockumentary' sitcoms that closely ape the format of reality shows, especially docusoaps with their emphasis on mundanity and eccentric characters (e.g. *Phoenix Nights, Summer Heights High, What We Do in the Shadows, People Just Do Nothing, The Office*). For Davis (2012), a key factor in their success is the emphasis on fame-seeking characters:

> *The mockumentary is able to take aim at reality*
> *television by presenting exaggerations of the genre's*
> *selfish, egotistical, often deluded personalities,*
> *who tend to labour under the illusion that fame*
> *is their destiny. Mockumentaries highlight the*
> *belief underscoring reality TV that the focus of the*
> *television camera promises fame and celebrity for*
> *ordinary people. (p. 97)*

However, there have also been many criticisms of mockumentary comedies. Although there is not room to expand on
these criticisms in detail, one key argument is that the jokes are
not always just at the expense of the TV format they mimic, but
at the groups represented, who are often portrayed as crude stereotypes reinforcing xenophobia, homophobia and other forms
of discrimination (Campbell, 2007; Hight, 2010; Mallett, 2010).

The Simpsons has parodied almost every genre of reality,
from talent shows, to historical lifestyle experiments, to *Wife
Swap*, to *Cops* – sometimes, using the voices of those involved
in the genre in real life. In a case of cross-show product placement, it even inspired a design challenge for *Project Runway*,
in which contestants designed dresses for Marge, with the
winning look featuring in an episode:

> MARGE: *I know you well enough to know that*
>   *this will work (opens coat to reveal*
>   *purple dress designed on* PR*).*
>
> HOMER: *Where did you get that dress?*
>
> MARGE: *Remember that sewing machine you*
>   *said I never use? Well I sold it and*
>   *bought this dress.*
>
> HOMER: *Wow, wow, that looks just like the dress*
>   *you wore on* Project Runway*!*

MARGE: *Shush, shush, shush.*

HOMER: *Oh,* right. *This looks like a dress from a local Springfield store.('Luca$', S25 E17, 2014).*

Even sci-fi adventure series *Doctor Who* has mimicked the genre, most notably in the episode 'Bad Wolf' (2005) in which the Doctor, Captain Jack and Rose find themselves trapped in the far future taking part against their will in robot-hosted versions of *What Not to Wear, Big Brother and The Weakest Link* as a satire on the pervasiveness of factual entertainment TV in the 2000s that now feels dated, following the cancellation of all three shows.

British writer and former TV critic, Charlie Brooker, has repeatedly returned to reality television as source material for his dystopian comedy-sci-fi/horror dramas. In *Dead Set* (2008), a group of zombies take over the *Big Brother* house. In a handy bit of cross-promotion (the shows aired on Channel 4 and E4, part of the same network), *BB* presenter, Davina McCall, and several former housemates make cameos in the show. Brooker said that whilst he thought people might watch because 'They're expecting half an hour of "I hate *Big Brother*!" ' (Jablonski, 2008), he saw the series more as a take-off of *24*. He explained the inspiration for the *Big Brother* setting:

> *And then one night I was watching* Big Brother *when another thought struck me. All zombie movies eventually boil down to a siege situation. What better place to hide than a fortified house thronged with cameras? Every person in the country must've fantasised at some point about what would happen if some terrible apocalypse occurred during a run of* Big Brother, *leaving the*

> *contestants oblivious. So that would be the starting*
> *point. (Brooker, 2008)*

Brooker's attention returned to reality in *Black Mirror* (2011-present) in several episodes, including 'Fifteen Million Merits', where currency, or 'merits' are earned through endless participation in different reality shows, 'The Entire History of You', where people's lives are constantly recorded and can be watched to 'prove' the reality of memories, and 'White Bear', where a convicted criminal is relentlessly followed and filmed as part of her punishment. Whilst these examples could be read as satire on reality TV, Brooker has distanced himself from that claim, saying of Fifteen Million Merits, for example:

> *although the contest at the heart at the story may*
> *look familiar, the episode is not a 'satire on talent*
> *shows'. It's more about the tainted surrounding*
> *air Bing and Abi have no choice but to breathe: it's*
> *about wanting something better than you currently*
> *have. (in* Radio Times *Team, 2011)*

As terrifying as *Black Mirror*'s take on reality TV is, however, it pales in comparison to an older programme, *Ghostwatch* (1992). Pre-empting paranormal exploration shows like *Most Haunted* by several years (Hill, 2011, p. 68), *Ghostwatch* was a fictionalised account of a TV crew, led by popular BBC presenter, Sarah Greene, visiting a house where a family claimed to be haunted by a poltergeist.

Although the programme was a drama, it had not been presented as such by the BBC. Broadcast on Halloween, the show presented itself as a 'live' broadcast and looked like factual TV in every way. Well-known factual TV personalities played themselves (alongside Greene were her presenter husband, Mike Smith, and veteran broadcaster, Michael Parkinson);

footage switched between Greene *in situ* at the family home and a studio set with Smith, Parkinson and a team of 'experts'; and a telephone bank for 'viewer calls' was set up, as commonly used in other live broadcast factual shows like *Crimewatch* – even using a real phone number adopted by many BBC shows.

As a young teen, I remember watching it, and assuming it was all happening for real. When the poltergeist activity started happening on-screen, represented through banging pipes and unusual shadowy presences, it was genuinely frightening – indeed, I was so scared, I went to bed part-way through! Although the programme descended into mayhem towards the end, exposing it as a clear fiction, many viewers (like myself) had switched off by this point, and over 20,000 calls were made to the phone line shown on screen complaining about the show as it went out.[3]

Of course, at school the next morning, *Ghostwatch* was the talk of the class, separating the hardcore who had stayed up for the whole programme from the rest of us who wimped out! Watching it all the way through became a common practice at sleepovers over the next couple of years, as a process of picking apart, and laughing at, the fictions, and at ourselves for being so easily duped!

Such was the negative response from viewers (including a minor moral panic, fuelled by the press claiming that a young man had taken his life as a response to the show – see Woods, 2017) that the BBC refused to repeat it, and it was only made available for home release in 2002 for the 10th anniversary.

What made *Ghostwatch* either very successful, or a complete disaster (depending on whether you perceive it as a sharp piece of horror and satire, or a tasteless attempt to dupe viewers) was the way it perfectly emulated the tropes of popular factual entertainment – or what we would now call 'reality TV'. Writer Stephen Volk explained how he designed the show to stylistically blend the modes of fact and fiction:

> *I really wanted to do a ghost story for television ... how do you get the authenticity on TV with the artificiality of drama? Could we tell a story using the language of live television rather than normal drama? The second thing was that there was the opportunity to be satirical about TV. In 1992 there was a blurring of the lines between TV and drama. Factual stuff was starting to look like fiction and vice versa. I was intrigued by the notion of the TV expert. We were the original fake news in a way: playing with the idea of trust. That came back to bite us in the bum because people trusted the BBC to tell them what was true and what was false. (in Earnshaw, 2017)*

Ghostwatch may have been deliberately designed to blur the boundaries between 'fact' and 'fiction', but sometimes the fictional excesses of parodied reality TV become a reality. *Most Haunted* and similar paranormal investigation shows take aspects of the *Ghostwatch* template in their investigation of the paranormal, and even comedy versions of reality television have proved prophetic – for example, sketch comedy *The Adam and Joe Show* (2001) parodied the time-travel reality genre (where people experiment with living as if they were in the past, e.g. *The 1900 House*) with their '*1980s' House*' sketch in which a family went back and lived with retro technology – only for this to become realised in further time-travel reality series such as *Electric Dreams* and *Back in Time For ...* when the 1980s (and 1990s!) were destinations for their participant families. Ricky Gervais's *Extras* also pre-empted entertainer Lionel Blair's time in the *Celebrity Big Brother* house by putting him in their fictional version seven years before he entered the real house.

Fictional representations of reality television, then, can tell us a lot about the way the genre is perceived. That there is a strong sense of satire in many representations, not only in sitcom and sketch shows but also within horror and drama, demonstrates the way the genre is often understood as lacking in seriousness. Most fictional representations play up the exaggerated style and eccentric characters found in many reality shows, and these are often combined with a sense of criticism of the genre's tropes and excesses – from its pervasiveness and ruthlessness, to the idea that it is exploiting and belittling its stars. There are moments of affection for the genre also present in some of these fictional takes – not least the presence of real presenters and personalities playing themselves. Ultimately, though, these fictional takes reveal the same anxieties that we have already seen pervade discussions of reality television – fears of surveillance, having to always perform 'good citizenship', concerns about the ideas of what is 'real' – and queries to what extent this matters.

WHY REALITY TV MATTERS TO AUDIENCES

There has been a lot of research into reality television audiences, conducted both by academics and by industry bodies – and, as you might expect, studies do not always ask the same things, nor provide the same results. As Carolyn Michelle (2009) points out, there are a whole range of audience responses to programmes, and some research, especially with children, suggests some audience members take reality shows at face value, rather than engaging in sustained critique of the shows and their relationship to them. It is also worth noting that those who contribute to research studies are more likely to have strong opinions, by virtue of agreeing to take part, and may also be performing a role of 'critical viewer' that they believe is expected of them. Nevertheless, there are several key recurring themes across the study of reality audiences that can give us some insight into why people watch reality shows, and what they think about them.

Whilst not all reality television shows have been successful, either critically or commercially, several high-profile examples have had extraordinary reach – attracting millions of viewers, receiving coverage in wider media, and becoming national, and even global, talking points.

As previously discussed in this chapter, however, their success in terms of reach, popularity and visibility does not mean they are necessarily always *liked*. The perceived lack of cultural value associated with the genre may mean people do not admit to liking – or even watching – these shows. Some audience research suggests that viewers who will often state that they do not watch reality television will reveal, when pressed, a range of experiences of watching different shows, and strong opinions on these programmes (Lundy, Ruth, & Park, 2008). In addition, viewers who do admit to regularly watching reality shows often express a sense of shame about the fact that they do:

> *I feel really stupid, I mean I am in college I should be smarter than that. I mean, I am 20 and I know I have a lot to learn but I usually like talking about something a little more intellectual than something like that. (Lundy et al., 2008, p. 219)*

If we think back to Bourdieu's discussion of class and taste, we can see how these might be factors influencing the way certain members of the audience approach reality TV. For example, in audience research with women from different class and ethnic groups, Skeggs, Thumin, and Wood (2008) noted that

> *Our middle-class participants also often assumed that the researchers would share with them the cultural attitude of derision towards 'reality' television, and indeed television per se, as a bad object (see also Seiter, 1990). That is not to say that these women did not watch and express pleasure in 'reality' television, but when asked to discuss particular programmes they did so by displaying their skill in holding the form at a distance ... They needed to show not only cultural detachment, but also cultural superiority to the bad object.*
> *(pp. 9, 11)*

In contrast to their working-class participants, who called programmes 'entertaining', these middle-class women often critiqued the programmes and were keen to display their sense of distaste for aspects of the genre, even as they admitted to watching and enjoying it – and even using its advice, such as the parenting tips found in the show *Supernanny* and its spin-off books. Allen and Mendick (2012) found very similar results in their study of youth reality audiences, where working-class respondents laughed at children behaving badly, or unclean houses, and middle-class viewers criticised working-class reality celebrities like Jade Goody, for lacking in talent and 'merit' (see also Chapter 5).

Viewers also tend to ascribe reality shows to an imagined hierarchy of what is 'good' and 'bad', according to the value they are perceived as having – audience opinions here often align with those of journalists, and are heavily influenced by a range of features, including the channel a show is broadcast on, its themes, title, format and aims. It does not necessarily follow that 'good' shows are those people choose to watch, and 'bad' those they do not, but the way audiences talk about the content of programmes and their reasons for watching changes according to the 'value' they assign to each particular show.

Participants in Lundy et al.'s research, for example, preferred shows that either focussed on learning skills, or offered a 'deserving' and uplifting reward to ordinary people who have worked hard, and engaged with the aims of the programme, and similar ideas occur in other studies:

> *He was quite common and quite like a grafter ...*
> *He made his way, and in the end he won it which is*
> *good. (Allen & Mendick, 2012, p. 470)*

> *I think she is very brave opening up her life and*
> *being so vulnerable. I so hope she finds it all*
> *worthwhile and is able to love herself. (Deller,*
> *2012a, p. 318)*

Shows typically seen as having low cultural value are those that are perceived as unethical, humiliating, sensationalist, exploitative, unrealistic, immoral or shallow (Bonner, 2013; Dovey, 2005; Hill et al., 2005), and viewers are often heavily critical of shows that seem to treat their participants and/or audience with contempt:

> *they have the women in these sports bras and little*
> *shorts so their stomachs are hanging out, and they*
> *have the men take off their shirts to get weighted,*
> *and they're just these little flimsy shirts, so why*
> *would they make them take off their shirts? I felt like*
> *it was a sensationalism aspect to really kind of go*
> *'Look how fat these people are' (Sender, 2012, p. 92)*

> *I thought these poor families, they were so exposed,*
> *these couples with difficulties in their relationships,*

> *everything was just wide open for the whole world*
> *to see and I thought that was terrible. (Skeggs et al.,*
> *2008, p. 10)*

There are also specific criticisms viewers make around the ethics of reality shows and concern for participants' wellbeing, a topic we will look at in more detail in Chapter 3.

One key theme in audience research (and one that links very closely to the aims of the genre) is the way reality shows allow viewers to gain some insight into other people's lives, experiences and feelings. This may serve a number of purposes, including: escapism, voyeurism, education and identification, as the following audience comments show:

> *as a viewer you can see yourself in that situation or*
> *you can say to yourself, if I was on that show this*
> *is what I would do. It is reality 'cause you can see*
> *yourself in it. (Lundy et al., 2008, p. 214)*

> *Some programmes really make me think. I remember*
> *a programme with a cancer patient being filmed and*
> *interviewed by her sister. This made me think: ooh!*
> *This could happen to me! (Biltereyst, 2004, p. 18)*

Getting to 'know' participants through seeing their lives and feelings played out on television often leads the audience to form a strong emotional connection with them, especially when the feelings shown are considered to be 'real', or the person showing their 'true' self.

> Big Brother. *I felt I knew the people in there, 'cos*
> *after a while, although there's cameras there, in the*
> *beginning they did all act up but you can't do it all*
> *the time ... And you get really close to the people,*
> *'cos you, like, get to know them. (Hill, 2005, p. 71)*

> *I like Dean the best because he appears to be the*
> *housemate who I presume is most like what he is in*
> *the real world. (Jones, 2003, p. 413)*

In some cases, this means empathising with their situations, although there are many examples where participants are judged and criticised for their behaviour, and often for wasting the 'opportunity' afforded to them by taking part in the programme:

> *There is a difference between being eager and*
> *aggressive for the job and being an overconfident*
> *raging diva … she is pushing the diva side! … We*
> *all saw the wicked witch come out in her weeks*
> *ago. (Michelle, 2009, p. 153)*

There can also be an element of schadenfreude in watching reality TV, especially when those being humiliated or receiving a form of comeuppance are seen as deserving that fate, whether by their actions on the reality show itself, or because they have been presented as having traits viewers dislike, such as laziness, entitlement or narcissism:

> *If the show has like 20 ridiculously hot girls*
> *who are all used to being pampered and are*
> *put outside in some extraordinary situation where*
> *they have to, like, shovel manure or something*
> *like that, it really amuses me. (Lundy et al., 2008,*
> *pp. 214–5).*

> *honestly … one of the best parts of watching [the*
> *show] is when … they show all the auditions and*
> *it's absolutely hilarious to watch these people who*
> *think they can sing and dance and they get up there*
> *and they don't … know what they are doing. (Hall,*
> *2006, p. 206)*

In this way, audiences often align themselves with the 'dominant reading' of the programmes (Hall, 1973), siding with the 'deserving' and approving of the improvement the reality show will have on their lives, whilst disapproving of those the show has cast as undeserving (Michelle, 2009; Tyler, 2013) and enjoying them receiving due 'punishment'. Whilst we might be tempted to see these viewers as more 'passive' than their critical counterparts, this is a rather simplistic understanding – audiences may not question the narratives because they reaffirm their pre-existing prejudices, and 'aesthetic dispositions' (a term coined by Bourdieu (1984) to describe the way our social and educational background teaches us to prefer particular people groups, views and tastes); or they may be deliberately choosing to 'switch off' their critical mode because they want to be entertained without engaging in the 'work' of critique.

Entertainment is, unsurprisingly, a core reason for watching reality TV, coming top of the list of viewer gratifications in studies by Nabi, Biely, Morgan and Stitt (2003) and Papacharissi and Mendelson (2007). The latter study argues that there is also a close correlation with how 'real' viewers perceive a show as being and how entertaining they think it is. The 'reality' of a show is not only judged by the participants and their behaviours and how authentic these feel, but also by audience speculation over how much the show has been edited by producers to create particular narratives rather than reflecting the 'reality' of what took place:

> *We only see what Channel 4 wants us to see.*
> *We only see extraordinary events rather than what*
> *people are usually like. It's an unreal situation.*
> *I don't follow the live action, I only look at*
> *the highlights on the web and Channel 4*
> *which are edited so (I) don't get a true reflection.*

> *You only get what makes good television. (Jones, 2003, p. 411)*

> *The producers of this show are desperate. It is among the lowest rated of all the summer shows. They need drama. What better way than to take someone who is in the lead and edit/spin/splice to create the drama they feel they need to increase their show's ratings. (Michelle, 2009, p. 157)*

Many viewers engage in a mixed mode of viewing where they shift between critiquing and accepting what is presented – as Michelle (2009) puts it,

> *at one moment they acknowledge features of textual construction such as the use of selective editing, but at other moments speak about the text as though it were documentary realism (p. 161).*

Unsurprisingly, viewers have strong responses to seeing people like them on reality television, especially viewers from marginalised and minority communities. The potential of seeing people like themselves presented in a positive light and revealing the challenges they go through can be seen as one of the key benefits of reality television.

> *As long as we're out there and we're being seen, somebody is being affected by that and somebody who sits down to watch* Queer Eye *or catches it unexpectedly, who is inclined to dislike us ... somebody out of thousands is gonna watch it and be like 'wait, maybe we misjudged'. (gay male interviewee in Sender, 2012, p. 90)*

Of course, the converse is also true, and viewers are also highly critical when they perceive their identity group is being portrayed badly, either through the way participants from that group present themselves, the way they have been edited, or both:

> *They'll get the most extreme priests/vicars they*
> *can find, and put them in a room of sceptics and*
> *edit it accordingly to portray the priests showing*
> *homophobic behaviour and saying lists of 'you*
> *shouldn'ts' all the time. (Deller, 2012a, p. 283)*

> *I just thought 'get her off because people are*
> *watching this now and they're gonna think*
> *that's what all black women are like'. (Sender,*
> *2012, p. 89)*

One core motivation for viewers is the opportunity to use reality television as a talking point. Several viewers watch to be part of a social experience involving friends, family and/or colleagues, often building mini-rituals around their viewing; this privileges these shows as 'must-see' TV that rewards live viewing as participation in the social space, and these shows then operate not only as pieces of entertainment but also as vehicles for social connection:

> Strictly Come Dancing ... *I think that is now*
> *the only time we sit down together as a family.*
> *(Ofcom, 2016, p. 9)*

As we will see in Chapter 6, this shared social experience is not restricted to being in the same location as the friends and family you are watching with, but may be facilitated through mobile phones and social media:

> *My wife's got a group chat called 'Great British*
> *Bakeoff' with all her family on it ... At the end of*
> *the series they'll delete that group off WhatsApp ....*

'See you next series!'. (Knowledge Agency/Ofcom, 2019, p. 25)

Group bonding over reality shows inevitably involves criticism of aspects of these shows, whether these criticisms are of individual personalities, or of the editing and production values. Indeed, this criticism is a core part of the appeal for many viewers, who engage in 'hate-watching' (Andrejevic, 2008; Gray, 2005) where they specifically watch shows in order to critique them. Gilbert (2019) notes reality TV lends itself to this practice because its structures often encourage us to make value judgements (p. 65), and because it is already seen as 'bad' TV – although she notes there are also audience communities that hate watch more 'prestigious' TV precisely because of the perceived importance attached to it by cultural commentators.

Audience members can also use the idea of critical viewing as a way of justifying their investment in the programmes – aware of their status as 'bad' cultural objects, viewers often explain their viewing in ways that demonstrate this knowledge, justifying watching either because they will be criticising it (usually, with others), or because it is the equivalent of wallpaper, something they can just 'switch off' from, even though they 'know' it is 'trash':

> Insider, Expedition Robinson*, well the docu soaps like, eh* Par påProv, Extreme Makeover, The Apprentice *... these are really the kind of programmes I watch because I want to relax and not think and maybe even gossip with friends the next day about how horrible they are. (Hill, Weibull, & Nilsson, 2005, p. 18)*

> *One knows it is not an investigative programme so you don't watch it with those eyes ... with easier*

eyes just to relax, more, something which is just,
sometimes I can think someone is stupid, or have a
laugh or think it's fun. (Hill et al., 2005, p. 34)

CONCLUSION

This chapter has outlined some of the key themes in the study
of reality television, and some of the reasons why it matters
to academics, audiences and the wider media industry. I will
revisit some of these themes in the following chapters, as we
begin to look in more detail at the genre's processes, personalities and content.

NOTES

1. https://www.ok.co.uk/celebrity-news/amy-hart-leave-love-
island-18296470

2. https://mepdf.com/heat-uk-20-july-2019/

3. https://www.ofcom.org.uk/__data/assets/pdf_file/0022/
149251/adults-media-lives-report.pdf

3

THE BUSINESS OF REALITY TV

In September 2016, it was announced that Love Productions, the makers of *The Great British Bake Off*, had failed to reach an agreement with the BBC for rights to future series, and the show would be moving to rival broadcaster Channel 4. The baking show had been a huge hit for the BBC. Launched on BBC Two in 2010, by its fourth series, it attracted over 7 million regular viewers, and was moved to BBC One for series five. By 2016's seventh series, it was attracting over 13 million viewers and was the most watched show on British television.[1]

Therefore, the sale to Channel 4, a channel that was unlikely to achieve the ratings seen on BBC One, was a huge shock to audiences and the press. Initial coverage focussed on the money involved in the deal, with Channel 4's £25 million offer triumphing over the BBC's £15 million. Love Productions were portrayed in the press as putting profit before programmes (Agius, 2016; Dixon, 2018), although Love Productions' Richard McKerrow offered a different take:

> *We really had no choice. I think* Bake Off *would have died if we hadn't moved … It was a decision made on ethical grounds and I include receiving*

> *a fair price as ethical. I think it is perfectly ethical*
> *to ask someone to pay you a salary for what you*
> *are doing. And yet there was this, 'All they want*
> *is money' like money is a grubby issue. It is a real*
> *issue. The move has been characterised as greedy*
> *producers going for the money. I say simply we did*
> *it to protect the format (cited in Palmer, 2018).*

Quickly following the announcement, presenters, Mel Giedroyc and Sue Perkins, and judge, Mary Berry, announced they would not be 'following the dough' to Channel 4, but co-judge, Paul Hollywood, decided to stay with the programme. Coverage of this largely presented Perkins, Giedroyc and Berry as loyal to the channel and Hollywood as following the money. Perhaps, the most hyperbolic of these was the *Daily Mail* (usually the BBC's most vocal critics – although they have tended to be equally antagonistic towards Channel 4) printing the masthead 'Sweet Loyal Mary ... and a Greedy Love Rat' – which manages to get in a handy reference to Love Productions and previous stories about Hollywood's extra-marital affairs in one line.

One of the core issues raised by the *GBBO* move was the relationship between programme and channel. Coverage of the move repeatedly spoke of how *GBBO* was a show that was 'very BBC'. Its brand of gentle humour mixed with baking education and its portrayals of a united nation reflect middle-class nostalgic ideals (Hall & Holmes, 2017) often associated with the BBC and its emotional connection to the nation as its 'Auntie'. To many people – journalists, audiences and those involved in the programme – this was not simply a matter of business, it was an affective issue.

Interestingly, the transfer of *The Voice UK* from the BBC to ITV a few months earlier did not receive the same degree of outcry. There had been a history of press criticism of the

BBC's acquisition of the format, claiming it did not meet its public service remit to be distinctive (a previous BBC talent show, *Fame Academy*, had received similar criticisms). That *The Voice* originated in Holland, from the creator of *Big Brother*, also played a role in it being treated as not fitting the BBC ethos (Goddard, 2018). However, the fact that a baking talent show is seen as having more cultural value than a singing talent show also reinforces a particular notion of taste.

GBBO's move is not an isolated example of a reality show move having an affective impact. Reality shows being sold to different networks is a common practice in many countries and viewers often have strong responses to this. For example, when *Project Runway* switched networks in the USA from Bravo to Lifetime, fans repeatedly criticised the move and held up every aspect of the show that they did not like as evidence that Lifetime had ruined the brand. When the show returned to Bravo in 2019, the network heavily promoted the idea that it was coming home, and even retooled the logo to read 'Bravo *Project Runway*' to emphasise that the brand would be taken care of once more. This was especially interesting given that the return to Bravo also marked the first series since the departure of host Heidi Klum and mentor Tim Gunn, the show's faces for its first 16 seasons. In their place, Bravo presented itself as the show's authority and star, as much as their replacements, Karlie Kloss and Christian Siriano.

SELLING REALITY WORLDWIDE

Whilst the previous examples are about format sales within domestic settings, reality is a global business. Major production companies no longer operate in one territory but have bases worldwide. For example, one of the most well-known global brands, Endemol Shine (the home of formats such as

Big Brother and *MasterChef*) is the parent company to over 120 'labels' (i.e. smaller production companies) in 23 countries (Endemol, 2019).

Reality franchises have been sold all over the world – there have been almost 80 versions of *MasterChef*, over 40 of *Strictly Come Dancing/Dancing With the Stars* and 70 iterations of *Got Talent*. Franchising programmes can be attractive to broadcasters because:

> *although multichannel television exists in most countries now, national broadcasting systems don't all have sufficiently strong production industries to create all the programming required. The format is useful here as it crucially offers the advantage of combining the adoption of an idea devised, and hence often 'proven', elsewhere with the possibility of local production, material and adaptation which has a greater chance of success with domestic audiences. (Holmes & Jermyn, 2004, p. 13)*

The process of franchising a show usually involves selling a format 'bible' outlining rules, templates, structures and production processes, providing branding materials and importing 'flying producers' from the parent company to assist in implementation and quality control (Singh & Kretschmer, 2012).

This does not mean that franchised versions are all identical – each home territory brings its own spin, and sometimes innovations from one international version are adopted by others – for example, whilst *MasterChef* originated in the UK, it was the Australian version that became the template for many of the global versions (Hill, 2019), and various innovations from different national *Big Brother* and *Dancing With the Stars* versions have spread to other territories.

International franchises also offer opportunities for personnel to cross nations, from former *Strictly Come Dancing* professionals who have found judging or dancing roles in international versions to judges who hop between franchises. For example, *Got Talent* and *X Factor* franchises from Simon Cowell's Syco production company have seen judges including Mel B, Louis Walsh, Dannii Minogue, Sharon Osbourne and Cowell himself transfer between different international versions.

In the last few years, the international market has not only involved traditional broadcasters but also streaming platforms. Amazon Prime, Netflix, Hulu and other operators are now as likely as traditional broadcasters to commission and purchase reality franchises. Netflix has been particularly active, commissioning shows like the *Queer Eye* reboot, cookery challenge show *Nailed It!* and makeover show *Tidying Up with Marie Kondo*. However, their core reality business is not in original formats, but in securing the rights to distribute archive shows and shows from different countries.

The rights business is complicated and leads to some viewer-frustrating outcomes. In the UK, *RuPaul's Drag Race* was initially shown on E4 for its first couple of seasons, but most viewers were introduced to the show through these and subsequent seasons being made available through Netflix. TruTV then took over screening new episodes for the 2015 series, followed by Comedy Central and VH1 gaining the rights to *All Stars* seasons and Netflix regaining the rights to be the 'main' series – and the UK adaptation of the show will be broadcast on BBC Three![2,3]

ADVERTISING, SPONSORSHIPS AND PRODUCT PLACEMENT

International sales are one way that reality shows can generate income for production companies, but they alone cannot finance production and development. Historically, television (outside of subscription services or publicly-funded broadcasters) has survived on the revenue from adverts.

Whilst advertising and sponsorship occur in all genres of programming, reality programming often has some of the most desirable slots, especially in the case of competitive reality and live broadcasts. Live shows such as *The X Factor*, ... *Got Talent* and *Dancing With the Stars* reward live viewing over watching via streaming and catch-up services, as if you do not watch as the show is broadcast, you miss out on the feeling of being part of a collective experience, including the opportunity to vote, and you may make yourself vulnerable to having the result 'spoiled' for you (for more on this, see Chapter 6). Because of the potential for audiences watching live, these shows can offer premium advertising slots. In the UK, for example, advert breaks during the *X Factor* live shows have often been when high-profile marketing Christmas campaigns have been launched – the seasonal adverts for retailers John Lewis and Marks and Spencer in particular are seen as moments of national excitement.

Advertising is often not only broadly targeted to the demographics likely to be watching the show (e.g. advertising make-up in shows with a large female audience; advertising family holidays during family viewing favourites) but also often very specifically targeted to the audience for a particular show. In these cases, adverts directly reference the show they are being shown within. This is especially the case online with the adverts that are integrated into many broadcasters' streaming platforms, and on official websites. A prominent example of this is *Love Island* UK. The advert breaks used on streaming platform ITV Hub almost exclusively reference the show. They include adverts for official show merchandise, for soundtrack albums, and adverts for other companies that use previous contestants as endorsers.

TV advertising occurs not only in the form of commercial breaks but also through sponsorship and product placement. Sponsorship involves a range of activities – most commonly a brief 'bumper' advert before the programme and during advert breaks, and ideally connected to the show in some way – UberEats' sponsorship of *Love Island*, for example, uses presenter, Caroline Flack, and voiceover artist, Iain Stirling, in the bumpers, and *Gogglebox* (which features people watching television from their sofas) has been sponsored by sofa outlets.

Product placement is where a brand or product advertises through being integrated into the content of a show, and the amount and nature of this varies within different countries. European countries adopted product placement much more recently than in the USA, for example, and in most European countries there are strict regulations about how it is used. For example, in many European shows, a placed product may appear in a more naturalistic way, such as when branded hair products are shown mingling with the rest of the domestic detritus in the *Big Brother* house, or when a particular brand of food is used in a cooking show – but, there may be no verbal attention drawn to these products by participants, hosts or voiceovers.

In the USA, product placement is a core aspect of a lot of reality programming, and often in very explicit ways. *American Idol* judges famously drank from cups with the Coca-Cola logo in some series, and these had to be blurred out when the show was shown in other countries where the sponsorship contract did not apply. *The Apprentice*'s tasks were often sponsored by different companies (including Post cereals, Gillette and Goodyear tyres). *Project Runway* partnered with several companies, providing everything used in the show from the obvious (fabrics, accessories and shoes, hair and make-up, sewing machines) to the bizarre (pens, water).

These product placements often caused amusement amongst fans who judged the health of the show by the quality of sponsoring brands, and by how sardonically Tim Gunn advised the contestants to use each year's chosen sponsor's accessory wall 'thoughtfully'.

There are also a range of other ways that the relationship between reality TV and commercial organisations can be maximised, such as the use of reality stars as brand endorsers and advertisers, and the development of reality television merchandise and tie-ins. These can range from the obvious – DVDs, tie-in books – to the more left field – board games, luggage, water bottles, food and drink.

THE ETHICS OF REALITY TELEVISION

In May 2019, news outlets covered the story of the family of a *Jerry Springer* subject, Blake Alvey, suing producers following his suicide. A few days later, UK broadcaster ITV announced that broadcasting and filming of long running talk show *The Jeremy Kyle Show* had been suspended, following the death of a participant. The initial statement announcing the suspension was opaque as to what had happened, but spoke at length about their duty of care measures:

> *ITV has many years' experience of broadcasting and creating programmes featuring members of the public and each of our productions has duty of care measures in place for contributors. These will be dependent on the type of show and will be proportionate for the level of activity of each contributor and upon the individual. All of our processes are regularly reviewed to ensure that they are fit for purpose in an ever changing*

> *landscape. In the case of* The Jeremy Kyle Show, *the*
> *programme has significant and detailed duty of care*
> *processes in place for contributors pre, during and*
> *post show which have been built up over 14 years,*
> *and there have been numerous positive outcomes*
> *from this, including people who have resolved*
> *complex and long-standing personal problems.*
> *(ITV, 2019)*

Unusually, the press release continued to describe their duty-of-care process before finally revealing the reason for the press release:

> *[E]veryone at ITV and* The Jeremy Kyle Show *is*
> *shocked and saddened at the news of the death of a*
> *participant in the show a week after the recording*
> *of the episode they featured in and our thoughts*
> *are with their family and friends. We will not*
> *screen the episode in which they featured. Given*
> *the seriousness of this event, ITV has also decided*
> *to suspend both filming and broadcasting of* The
> Jeremy Kyle Show *with immediate effect in order*
> *to give it time to conduct a review of this episode of*
> *the show, and we cannot comment further until this*
> *review is completed. (ITV, 2019)*

Over the rest of the day, the media was rife with speculation about what had happened – it soon transpired that 63-year old Steve Dymond had taken his life following the recording of an episode in which he failed a lie detector test.[4,5] Releasing a press statement about their duty of care measures before any details about the incident might seem premature on behalf of the broadcaster, but Dymond's death came at an unfortunate time for the broadcaster. Two months earlier, Mike Thalassitis, a former star of ITV show *Love Island*

(and also E4's *Celebs Go Dating*), died by suicide, and nine months prior to that, the death of another former *Love Island* star, Sophie Gradon, was also widely speculated to be a suicide.

The *Jeremy Kyle* and *Love Island* deaths were presented in the media as symptomatic of a wider malaise affecting reality television, generating sensational headlines calling for axe and reform (although the press conveniently tended to sidestep their own role in representing reality stars negatively):

> *THIRTY-EIGHT people have died in suspected suicides linked to reality TV shows, the* Sun on Sunday *can reveal. Despite this telly bosses are allegedly allowing vulnerable people on screens with little or no support. (Spencer, 2019)*

Former participants, production staff and audience members from these and other shows were called upon to give interviews to shed the light on the problems of the industry:

> *One thing's for sure, when the producers of Love Island sold us 'the dream', they never warned us about the reality we could face …. I'm trying to get to grips with what's just happened. A 26-year-old guy. My friend. He couldn't go on. This isn't a show. This is the real thing …. I know that there are many others who left the show and were hit with depression following a baptism of fire that they never anticipated, were not properly warned about, and then were left to their own devices to deal with when the sun set on the season. (*Love Island *contestant, Jonny Mitchell, 2019)[6,7]*

> *I know quite a few people who've appeared on shows like this, and they all have a horrible story*

> *to tell. They've become alcoholics, turned to drugs,*
> *lost themselves to depression or anxiety, developed*
> *eating disorders or pursued obsessive, attention-*
> *seeking behaviour on social media. Of course,*
> *these tendencies existed before – the problems*
> *weren't created by programme makers, but they*
> *were certainly made worse. The toxic nature of*
> *reality TV, the manipulation by producers who*
> *are little more than puppeteers, and the instant,*
> *snarling effects of fame, can have a devastating*
> *effect …. I was an anxious, lonely and sad*
> *young girl with a crippling eating disorder and*
> *a family history of mental health problems ….*
> *I crumbled in front of the nation, exhibiting*
> *increasingly erratic behaviour …. How I passed*
> *the psychological assessments to get on the show*
> *continues to baffle me. I should never have been*
> *allowed on. (*Big Brother *contestant Caroline*
> *Wharram, 2019)*[8]

However, the concentration of these suicides in a short space of time caused a minor moral panic (Cohen, 2002; Geiringer, 2019). In which several parties-politicians, journalists, audience members, former participants and staff members-called for tighter regulation of the sector and the British government announced plans for a select committee to investigate duty of care in the reality sector (DCMS, 2019).

ITV, no doubt already sensitive to the accusations around *Love Island* (which was due to return a few weeks after Dymond's death) were quick to act upon the Jeremy Kyle scandal and permanently cancel the talk show. They announced that the upcoming fifth series of *Love Island* would have more emphasis on psychological support and aftercare for those involved. Unsurprisingly, given its status as a ratings juggernaut, they made no attempt to cancel the upcoming series.

As tragic as any suicide is, it is difficult to say whether or not the reality television process played a role in people's decision to take their lives. 38 (the figure quoted in many tabloid accounts) suicides out of the hundreds of thousands of reality show participants is statistically small. It is also worth pointing that newspapers are happy to put the blame on television programmes and their production without acknowledging the role they themselves play in the treatment of reality show participants. There is an irony in seeing *The Sun* and *Daily Mail* criticising reality shows for the treatment of participants whilst at dissecting the domestic lives, appearances and personalities of reality stars on their own websites!

The UK government's initiative to look into reality television is by no means the only political intervention into reality programmes. Alongside Kraidy's accounts of state intervention in reality TV in the Arab world, in 2017 the popular Chinese show *The Rap of China* was cancelled, and hip-hop artist, GAI, removed from reality talent show *Singer* (formerly, *I Am Singer*) when the Chinese government announced a ban on hip-hop being represented on TV.

THE ETHICS OF REALITY TV

Although recent stories about suicides have put the genre in the media and political spotlight (at least in the UK), the idea of reality TV as unethical and potentially abusive is nothing new – it has been a concern of journalists, authors and some academics from the beginning. Even one of the most respected formats, … *Up* (in which participants are visited for life updates every seven years) has come in for criticism over its intrusion into participants' lives from childhood, and especially for its portrayal of Neil, who struggled with homelessness and mental illness (Kilborn, 2010).

Many former reality stars have given confessional interviews over the years in which they detail the difficulty of readjustments to life during, and after, after the reality show (Brookstein, 2015; Kaur, 2007). A typical example is former *X Factor* contestant, Christopher Maloney's, description of anxiety and depression following negative representation on the show and in the press:

> *My paranoia went into overdrive … I did not know what lay ahead and I am not talking about the shattered pieces of a possible career. I was barely functioning minute to minute … the stories about me had broken me … My shakes were terrible and almost continual. I rarely washed …. My mind had been attacked and my body had shut down. (Maloney, 2018, ch. 22)*

Several former *Big Brother* contestants have argued that the 'talk of doom' they were given before entering the programme, designed to alert them to the potential hazards of reality fame, did not cover the situations that they would eventually encounter:

> *The talk of doom was rubbish. They didn't tell me anything that I hadn't already thought of, for example, the press may talk to your family …. They didn't tell me I could have death threats …. They didn't warn me that people make up stories about you. The people will judge me when they don't even know me, that I could potentially be the victim of the verbal and physical abuse …. The one thing I wish they had told me was, 'once we're finished*

with you, we are going to have nothing to do with you'. (Antwi in Kaur, 2007, p. 41)

I really resent it when people say, well, you should have known the pitfalls, you were warned. And you had watched previous series ... What I've gone through could only have happened to me .... I am unique to me, no one from my culture has ever gone on Big Brother *and so when they give you the talk of doom, how could they warn me about how Zimbabwe would take it if I wore a bikini? And besides, they didn't warn me that going on would have the potential to make people hate me – send death threats – so I wouldn't be able to go back to my own country. If I had been warned [about] attributed as (Musambasi in Kaur, 2007, p.45)*

There is no one consistent approach amongst the amount within the industry as to psychological support, preparation and aftercare for participants. Of those I interviewed, some received no support at all, whilst others had access to a psychologist throughout the whole process and beyond. Claudia, who took part in two different shows, received no aftercare at all. For others, psychologists were involved, or productions offered a clearer advice and aftercare package. In a programme focussing on trans people's journeys, a psychologist was involved in all stages of the process:

He was working for the benefit of us, the contributors, not them .... He always made it clear from day one that if I need him before or after – I still have his number in my phone – don't be afraid to contact him. The documentary I was involved in, I think they realised there was a high suicide rate in

> *the trans community and from day one they were*
> *very responsible. If they weren't, I don't think I'd*
> *have had anything to do with it. (Observational*
> *participant)*

A family featured in an observational documentary had a similar experience, not only of having psychological support but also some media training:

> *Well the BBC were good in that, was it before*
> *the filming or before, we had a psychologist come*
> *round and make sure [we] were OK .... And the*
> *BBC Press Office gave us a contact number so if*
> *there were any comments in the papers or we had*
> *any trouble with people contacting us after the*
> *documentary wanting interviews and things they*
> *could contact them. They suggested that we didn't*
> *do any interviews for sort of* Hello *magazine or* Sun
> *or something like that because they would twist it*
> *nicely, but they organised the* Telegraph *interview,*
> *that was good, but yeah, [we had] a good working*
> *relationship with them. (Observational participants)*

A participant in *The Great British Bake Off* not only expressed the show's duty to participants but also felt that, as a participant in a popular brand, they had a duty to the show:

> *In the psychological assessment, they covered things*
> *like how are you going to cope with people coming*
> *up to you in the street or in the supermarket and*
> *so on, and she also asked me what will you do if*
> *no-one ever recognises you? ... You do realise that*
> *you are carrying the responsibility of a much-loved*
> *series, so you're not going to behave in a certain way.*

There is an interesting tension at work when we consider whether or not reality television provides its participants with enough support for their mental, physical and emotional well-being, given that the ethos of many reality shows is that they are there to improve these very things through the intervention of a makeover, social experiment or journey into the self (see Chapter 4). As Hawkins (2001) puts it:

> *Ethics have become entertainment ... there is*
> *the emergence of a whole range of new formats,*
> *from docusoaps to reality TV to tabloid talk,*
> *where everyday ethical dilemmas are very often*
> *the source of conflict and content. Growing*
> *amounts of television programming now involve*
> *examinations of ways to live: information about*
> *the care and management of the self, explorations*
> *of the tensions between collective versus self-*
> *interest. (pp. 412–413)*

One key ethical concern about reality television is whether or not participants are represented 'fairly' in both the programmes and in the wider media and audience discourse surrounding them. One of my interviewees took part in a social experiment programme and was highly critical of not only her edit, but by the way she was treated in the rest of the media:

> *I hated it, it was really really upsetting. I used to*
> *listen to Radio 4 till I turned it on one morning and*
> *found [presenter] just ripping into me and saying*
> *all sorts of horrible things and getting it completely*
> *wrong actually because she was quoting [another*
> *participant] ... and you'd think that there would be*
> *a difference wouldn't you in the way something's*
> *presented in what* The Sun *would put and maybe*

> *what* The Observer *would put but actually there*
> *was no difference at all.*

Controversies about reality television are not confined to representation or psychological support but occur around the activities involved in reality shows. One recurring concern is of the bullying, harassment and ostracisation that can occur in these shows. There have been countless examples of sexism, racism, homophobia and other prejudice within reality shows – some even make a feature of this and use it as a core part of their narrative (e.g. living with the enemy, other examples). Occasionally, this behaviour can lead to the eviction of participants for breaking show rules, but often situations are allowed to go on for some time to ramp up the drama, as well as providing opportunity for reconciliation and forgiveness for those involved.

Sometimes, this behaviour upsets viewers and commentators so much that they feel obliged to intervene on behalf of the contestants, especially when they perceive the programme makers are stoking these situations for good television, rather than intervening. Dutch reality show *The Golden Cage* was heavily criticised for a format that seemed to reward bullying, for example, and domestic violence charity Women's Aid issued a statement expressing concern when a *Love Island* contestant was accused of exerting controlling behaviour to the woman he was paired with. UK communications watchdog Ofcom regularly receives complaints from viewers about the treatment of reality television participants – reality shows made up five of its ten most complained about shows in 2018 (Ofcom, 2018) although they rarely find that programmes have fallen foul of industry guidelines.

There is also the ethical question of whether or not particular programmes should be made. In 2014, my hometown of Grimsby, along with the Welsh town of Merthyr Tydfil, protested the news that name of production company Keo were looking to film episodes of their *Skint* series in the towns. Following the uproar from Birmingham residents about their portrayal in *Benefits Street,* and Scunthorpe residents about their representation in *Skint's* first series, officials and residents of Grimsby and Merthyr Tydfil were concerned about the impact *Skint* could have on their reputations and protested loudly to Keo to cancel filming plans (Pidd, 2014). You may not be surprised to learn that both towns were, indeed, featured in *Skint* despite these protests.

THE ETHICS OF REALITY LABOUR

The issues of ethics and fair treatment hint at one of the most complex issues in the production of reality television – that of labour. Whilst there are several reasons for the reality show boom, one key factor highlighted by many authors is that they are significantly cheaper to produce than other genres in terms of the technical and material elements of production, and also personnel costs.

Several authors and argue that one of the catalysts for reality's success was the 1988 Writers' Guild of America (WGA) strike. With writers on strike for 22 weeks, networks were desperate to fill airtime, and during this period, Fox greenlit *Cops*:

> *This unscripted show, which required no actors'*
> *salaries and boasted extra low production costs.*
> *Indeed, much of the cinema verité feel of reality*
> *programming was pioneered by the use, in* Cops,
> *of handheld cameras to capture real police officers*
> *as they pursued their more action-oriented*
> *assignments. (Ross, 2014, p. 31)*

Cops' dispensing of a writing team proved an inspiration for the TV industry, keen to save money wherever possible. It was followed by several reality shows that did away with writers, instead seeing producers as 'editors, who patch together chunks of real life' (Ross, 2014, p. 31). The 2007–2008 WGA strike again saw a boom in reality-style programming, and union arguments that many of the people working on reality shows were, indeed, writers and should be treated as such, were roundly dismissed by the industry (Essany, 2008; Ross, 2014) – although it should be noted that practices in the industry vary in different countries and from programme to programme in terms of the acknowledgement of writers.

Another key area of cost-cutting in reality shows is the reliance (in all but the celebrity-focused formats) on ordinary people. Even where celebrities are involved as presenters and experts, they usually comprise a small portion of the people on-screen, with most of the work of creating the televised content in the hands of the participants. There is a lot of variety in the industry as to whether or not participants receive financial compensation, but it is common for people to only receive a nominal daily sum, equivalent to jury service, even in the most generous of examples. Generally, there is an expectation that participants are rewarded sufficiently by experience and exposure:

> *the prospect of free self-promotion on a wide*
> *broadcasting platform is considered to be an*
> *adequate form of compensation – it is a potentially*
> *more lucrative asset in the attention economy than*
> *the fixed, or measurable, wages of industrialisation.*
> *(Ross, 2014, p. 35)*

Even when there is a possibility for financial gain, it is not always taken up. For example, some reality shows offer participants the chance to take home a portion of prize money in exchange for leaving the show early. Those who take it may benefit financially, but often at the expense of the hit to their reputation in terms of audience opinions, or their popularity with fellow competitors. For those who turn down such opportunities, they often cite reasons of personal integrity and wanting to gain from the reality experience, such as in the case of *Big Brother* USA, where several housemates were offered up to $50,000 to leave early and refused:

> *all of them claimed that the experience of the* Big Brother *house was worth more to them than the certainty of taking home the $50,000. Cassandra, the houseguest he was voted out that week, told the show's host on the night it she was banished that she had no regrets about turning down the cash: for me it was a question of integrity, I didn't want to be bought, I didn't want to sell my soul. If I took the $50,000 I'd be saying that's what the experience was worth, and it was priceless. (Andrejevic, 2004, p. 145)*

The ethical issues around reimbursement for participant labour are rarely debated in the press, perhaps due to there being equally problematic labour standards in journalism, where there has also been a culture of exploiting free labour for the 'experience'. Entertainment sites like *Digital Spy* and *E!* occasionally run features on what reality stars are paid, but these are not presented as investigative pieces or calls for reform, but more as lightweight listicles full of humour:

> *[on naked dating show* Naked Attraction*] You'd think getting your kit off on national television in pursuit of love would be deserving of a hefty lump sum, but apparently the prestige of revealing*

> *your meat and two veg (or lady garden) for all and*
> *sundry to feast their eyes upon is more than enough*
> *.... YOU DON'T GET PAID IF YOU'RE ON*
> *THE SHOW. TBH, if we were looking to make a*
> *bob or two,* Naked Attraction *wouldn't be the one*
> *for us anyway. (Robinson, 2018)*

There are some instances where participants can receive substantial payments, but this is usually reserved for people cast in long-running shows, or who return to franchises (Bricker, 2018). The general expectation is that reality stars' opportunities to make money come after the shows have finished through public appearances and product endorsements, or through entering the realm of celebrity reality formats (see Chapter 5).

Even audiences engage in acts of labour for these shows through voting (which is often paid for through the phone bill) and engaging in conversation and, thus, promotion on social media – all without the companies paying for this interaction and publicity (Andrejevic, 2004, 2008).

WHEN REALITY TV DIES

One aspect of reality TV that is sometimes overlooked is what happens when it ends. Most television shows tend to have a shelf life – some are cancelled after a single season, whilst others continue as long as ratings are strong enough or they are making sufficient revenue in advertising and sponsorship to keep the brand lucrative. Hundreds of reality shows have come and gone – occasionally, they have been axed due to controversy (as with *The Jeremy Kyle Show*) but most are simply not re-commissioned and disappear without a big fanfare to send them off.

Some brands, such as *American Idol* and *Dancing On Ice* (UK), are the reality TV equivalent of zombies, having been killed off only to be resurrected a few years later. Some reality shows shamble on, seemingly unkillable. The *X Factor* UK is still broadcasting, 15 years after its launch, despite endless press speculation for the last several years about its declining ratings.

But perhaps the most interesting case study of the death of a reality show is the granddaddy of franchises, *Big Brother*. There have been over 50 international variations since the 1999 Netherlands original, but fewer than 20 survive at the time of writing. The Dutch *Big Brother* was an early casualty. It had a zombie existence – it was first cancelled in 2002 following its fourth series, was then reprised for two further runs in 2005–2006, cancelled again, then rebooted as *Secret Story* (the name of several international *Big Brother* variants) in 2011 before disappearing once more.

The UK version has a similar history of cancellations and reboots. Following the Shilpa Shetty versus Jade Goody incident in *Celebrity Big Brother* (2007), the spin-off was put on ice for until 2009. In 2010, Channel 4 announced their plans to retire the franchise altogether. The final series was approached as a finale in the same way long-running drama and comedy series often celebrate their final episodes. Promotional campaigns featured a Big Brother funeral, attended by a host of former housemates attending a burial service. The final 'civilian' series was immediately followed by *Ultimate Big Brother*, an all-stars variant bringing back memorable civilian and celebrity housemates.

However, *Big Brother* as a brand proved too big to die, with rival broadcaster Channel 5 purchasing the rights. It brought the Celebrity show back in 2011 and the civilian show a year later. Channel 5 presented its *Big Brother* as a continuation of the franchise, rather than a reboot. Past contestants from C4 became regular guests on C5 spin-off show *Big Brother's Bit on the Side*. However, in 2018, the series was cancelled once more.

In an unexpected turn of events, the National Trust, a British charity that maintains sites of historical interest, offered the public the opportunity to tour the *Big Brother* house in 2013, presenting it as a site of cultural importance. However, almost immediately after the 2018 series ended, the house was demolished – a brutal symbol of it no longer being important.

Still, demolition is perhaps a kinder end than that which befell the Australian *Big Brother* house. *BB* Australia is yet another iteration of the show that underwent multiple deaths – its Network Ten version was axed in 2008 (following several controversies), before the Nine Network broadcast its own version from 2012 to 2014. In the interim period between Ten and Nine's versions, the house was turned into a tourist attraction (befitting its location on the site of the Dreamworld theme park) and was made available to hire for private functions. The show finally ended in 2014, but the empty house remained *in situ*.

In 2019, a story went viral about urban explorer and YouTuber MuiTube (https://www.youtube.com/watch?v=JCKgMYJ9EJY) uploading footage of the abandoned set. Coverage of the story positioned the show as a curious cultural relic, with a sense of nostalgia combined with an awareness of its 'trashiness':

> *Let Us Revisit The Empty, Rotting Carcass Of The Iconic 'Big Brother' House … the house has both metaphorically and literally been left to rot ….*
> *It's a fascinating relic of reality TV long-gone ….*
> *The video — an exercise in hauntology — quickly gained 300,000+ views on the weekend, as it turns out nostalgia, cultural cringe and a vague eeriness are all you need to go viral. (Richards, 2019)*

> *The show gifted us with many iconic moments*
> *such as Sara Marie's bum dance and Merlin's silent*
> *protest .... RIP* Big Brother. *You probably won't be*
> *missed but you'll always be remembered. (Fry, 2019)*

A few days before this book went to press, the empty Australian BB house was destroyed by fire.

Even in the territories mentioned, *Big Brother* may still return from the dead. Endemol recently produced a new, pan-national, iteration of the eye logo used in several versions (most notably the UK, where every series was marked with a new 'eye') to mark the show's 20 years, and re-launched social media accounts for some of its axed franchises.

CONCLUSION

The industry surrounding reality television is big and complex – and I have only scratched the surface of the key issues facing it here. However, in a media climate still reeling from #MeToo and other abuse scandals, it is unlikely that the debate over the ethics of reality TV's production will go away any time soon – and we may see more franchises dismantled in the wake of investigations. However, the industry can sometimes have a kneejerk reaction to these crises, sacrificing a few scapegoats rather than dealing with sector-wide practices of exploitation and cost-cutting. After decades of asking its subjects to submit to processes of surveillance and improvement, perhaps it is time for the industry to turn the gaze upon itself.

NOTES

1. https://www.ofcom.org.uk/__data/assets/pdf_file/0021/102756/adults-media-lives-2016.pdf

2. https://www.eonline.com/uk/news/1015779/rupaul-s-drag-race-all-stars-crowns-2-winners-and-fans-are-freaking-out

3. https://www.gaytimes.co.uk/culture/118640/heres-how-former-drag-race-contestants-reacted-to-the-all-stars-4-finale/

4. https://www.itv.com/presscentre/press-releases/statement-itv-regarding-jeremy-kyle-show

5. https://www.independent.co.uk/news/media/tv-radio/jeremy-kyle-show-cancelled-steve-dymond-episode-suicide-death-itv-a8915236.html

6. https://www.thesun.co.uk/tvandshowbiz/8705713/love-island-mike-thalassitis-sophie-gradon-suicide-reality-tv/

7. https://www.theguardian.com/commentisfree/2019/mar/19/mike-thalassitis-love-island-death-reality-tv

8. https://www.dailymail.co.uk/news/article-6843139/Ex-Big-Brother-star-Caroline-Wharram-mentally-fragile-not-allowed-show.html

4

WHAT HAPPENS IN REALITY TV?

In 2009, an audition clip from *Britain's Got Talent* became a worldwide viral sensation. It achieved close to 30 million views, was covered by news and entertainment outlets the world over, made an instant superstar of its subject and its impact is still felt over a decade later.

It can be easy to forget that by 2009, talent formats like Idol, The *X Factor* and … *Got Talent* were long established in the schedules of broadcasters all over the world whilst they were popular with audiences, they were no longer seen as innovative or particularly remarkable. And then, this landmark TV moment happened.

At first, it seems like a standard piece of audition footage that could have been drawn from any talent show. Quirky music floods the soundtrack as we are introduced to a middle-aged woman with slightly unkempt greying hair wearing an unflattering beige dress and eating a white bread sandwich. In her broad Scottish accent, she introduces herself as Susan Boyle, 'nearly 48' and jokes with presenters, Ant and Dec, that she is in a 'fighting mood'. She talks about being single, 'never been married, never been kissed' and living alone with her cat. Viewers trained on reality talent shows knew the drill with this kind of auditionee – a deluded figure of fun who would get on the stage, humiliate themselves and provide fodder for judges and audience members to laugh at.

Boyle struts on to the *Britain's Got Talent* audition stage to some (presumably, ironic) whistles from the crowd, swivels her hips at the judges as a joke, and we cut to judge Piers Morgan looking aghast. As she says that her dream is to be 'a professional singer', the camera cuts to a girl in the crowd rolling her eyes. Boyle tells Simon Cowell she wants to be as famous as Elaine Paige, and the crowd laugh.

And then, she sings.

The audience whoop and the judges' jaws drop as they hear her near-flawless delivery of 'I Dreamed a Dream' and presenter Ant McPartlin wags his finger at us down the camera lens and scolds 'Youse didn't expect that, did you?'

And we did not. The viral success of Boyle's audition clip was precisely down to the way it subverted the audience's expectations. Years of 'comedy' auditions on talent shows – especially those involving Simon Cowell – had trained the audience to believe no-one who looks or acts like Boyle could possibly be talented. The presence of joke acts in talent shows, at first seen as part of their appeal, had been coming in for criticism by audiences and commentators for exploiting the vulnerable and potentially mentally ill (although we could argue that some of these concerns were a little patronising towards the participants, assuming they were not in on the joke), as well as being repetitive and predictable.

And here came Susan Boyle to seemingly smash the stereotypes and challenge our perceptions. On the surface, it might seem to be a classic tale of not judging a book by its cover – rebuking the audience for judging Boyle's appearance and personality before hearing her sing (even though this is precisely what these shows had taught us to do). But the more significant message underlying the audition is to challenge the audience's perception of the talent show as formulaic and reinforce the idea of it as a meritocratic process in which talent will win out.

Boyle's audition, even a decade later, is regarded as something of a landmark moment in reality television – partly because of its global spread and harnessing of social media (which I will return to in Chapter 6), but mostly because it was able to capitalise on several years of viewers around the world being used to the *Idol*, *Got Talent* and *X Factor* franchises, so that it could take that familiarity, subvert it and restate the case for reality television being able to find extraordinary talents in seemingly ordinary people. It could therefore justify its own existence, whilst also acting as a rebuff to critics of its comedy auditions format, with this clip demonstrating that true 'stars' will always shine through, and their personality and appearance need not be a barrier. This logic is, of course, part of the marketing gimmick for the more recent talent show *The Voice*, in which judges do not see performers before they hear them.

When the 2019 series of *Britain's Got Talent* launched, its second episode revisited this landmark moment – as new auditionees lined up to meet judges, we were treated to Boyle singing 'I Dreamed a Dream'. Instead of coming on making awkward jokes, Boyle strode on to stage, in silence save for the authoritative click of her heels. She was groomed and confident, her hair now sleek with honeyed highlights, wearing a glamorous sequinned frock that represented an upgrade of her audition piece. Boyle sang to the waiting auditionees as proof that the dreams presented by the reality show can come true, and Cowell came and joined her on stage: 'still got the magic, Susan, haven't you?' Ant and Dec reminded us that it was the 10th anniversary of her audition, and we launched into the auditions with judge Alesha Dixon saying 'let's find the next one!'

Alongside Boyle's return, the 2019 *BGT* series was notable for Ant McPartlin resuming his presenting duties. McPartlin is part of a longstanding presenting duo with Declan Donnelly. The pair rose to fame in the early 1990s as actors in teenage TV show Byker Grove. After leaving the show, they had a brief career as pop stars (firstly marketed as their characters PJ and Duncan, before being rebranded as Ant and Dec), before making the transition to television presenting (Bennett, 2011; Bonner, 2011). They have become synonymous with broadcaster ITV in particular, presenting many of its biggest reality shows, including *Pop Idol* and *I'm a Celebrity... Get Me Out of Here*, and have been the presenters of *Britain's Got Talent* since its launch.

In 2018, however, McPartlin's image as the loveable boy next door took a big hit when he was convicted of drink-driving, revealed his struggle with drug and alcohol addiction, and underwent a very public break-up with wife Lisa (herself a minor celebrity). He stood down from presenting commitments, leaving Donnelly to helm the 2018 series of *Britain's Got Talent* solo, a first for the presenter – Ant and Dec's brand image has always centred around them as a partnership (Bennett, 2011).

Susan Boyle, too, has experienced a fame journey far more troubled than what we see in the celebratory headlines of her global fame and multimillion selling records. She was famously admitted to hospital for mental health treatment after losing the *BGT* 2009 final to dance troupe Diversity (several members of this group remain high-profile celebrities in the UK, seemingly proving that it was less a case of Boyle 'losing' undeservedly and more a case of the show producing two major talents), and there have been numerous tabloid stories over the years about her struggles with the money, pressure and trappings of fame (Ross, 2014).

The celebration of Boyle and McPartlin in the 2019 series glossed over the struggles they both had, and presented the reality show not as a potential factor in their troubles, but as a place of safety and victory, a community in which they thrived.

This chapter is all about the storylines, structures and characters of reality television and I have chosen to open it with this example because it highlights many of the themes we will be exploring: the use of standard templates and structures for reality shows, coupled with the occasional moment where these 'break' in order to prove their authenticity; the types of personality involved – not only as participants but also judges and presenters; the storylines and journeys established for different characters, and the idea that reality television sees itself not only as entertainment, but as a vehicle to change people's lives.

REALITY TV CHARACTERS

Reality shows offer the opportunity for people from a wide range of backgrounds to appear on television. We see this most clearly in formats that involve multiple participants such as social experiments and competitions, with casts often comprised of people of different ages, ethnicities, sexualities, abilities, religions, occupations and backgrounds. Despite this apparent diversity, however, these participants are often represented according to a series of stock character types.

As we saw in Chapter 2, there can be character types that are closely aligned with cultural stereotypes (e.g. the scheming bitch, the scrounger, the spoilt rich kid, the screaming queen), but there are also a range of character types that relate to the storylines of particular shows. Sometimes, it may be that people are cast specifically to fill these niches, and at other times it is likely that the niche is chosen for them during the process of filming and editing.

Most obviously, there are hero characters who we root for. In competitive formats, these contestants usually win; in non-competitive formats, they are the characters the camera focuses on most closely. Their story arcs usually follow a classic hero's journey structure where we see them battling against struggles (either internal, external or both) to overcome and achieve a form of victory, either in the form of a prize, or in terms of personal growth. However, even though not every reality participant is the 'hero' of their show, most of them experience this kind of journey to some degree, as we will see later in the chapter.

There are also villains. Most villains are cast in this role because of the ways they deviate from the reality show rules, whether through breaking an established show rule (think *Project Runway* series one's Kara Saun bringing in luxury shoes she had been given as a favour, or *Big Brother* UK series one's 'Nasty' Nick Bateman who was caught writing down names for nominations), or breaking a social 'rule' by being arrogant rather than humble, being talentless rather than talented (or, at least, presented as such). Other villains can be those who have committed more egregious offences such as bullying, harassment or violence.

In addition to these, there will be contestants who act as (grand)parents to the rest of the group, and those who act as the 'baby'; the clowns who are there primarily to entertain; the 'triers' who are not yet ready to achieve hero status, and 'fodder' or 'filler' contestants who are edited as having minority roles in the series and receive less airtime than bigger personalities and those who are more demonstrably talented and capable.

Sometimes, it is clear from the first time we meet the participants who will fill which role, and, at other times, journeys emerge over the course of series. In competitive formats, for example, it is not always obvious from the early episodes who the winner will be (and, at times, when it is, audiences tend to complain about predictability!)

People who take part in reality shows are often aware that these programmes trade on easily identifiable character types and they sometimes construct a persona to get themselves noticed:

> *I played a character when I was on there… I knew I had to be the gay stereotype that was on the front of the papers every day. And I did my job well. I played the game. (X* Factor *contestant Rylan Clark-Neal in Jonze, 2019)*

> *They ask you to describe yourself and say how you think other people see you …. Some woman in the Ladies had just said she thought I was a 'ghetto princess'. I thought that sounded pretty good, so when it came to recording the video, that was how I presented myself. (*Big Brother *participant Aisleyne Horgan-Wallace, 2009, p. 192)*

When it comes to casting reality shows, 'some populations are more prized than others' (Mayer, 2014, p. 61), with white heterosexuals aged 18–35 and gay men more likely to be cast than people from other backgrounds. However, the casters Vicki Mayer interviews for her chapter exploring this process argue that it is hard to sometimes find willing participants from minority backgrounds as 'Contrary to the popular myth, not everyone wants to be on television' (Mayer, 2014, p. 61).

MEET THE MENTORS

One staple of many (although not all) reality formats is the mentor, judge or expert. Sometimes, these roles are combined, as in The *X Factor*, where judges each mentor a category and share their expertise, although they also utilise guest experts and mentors by bringing in pop stars to 'assist' at different stages of the competition. At other times, different people take these roles – in *Project Runway*, for example, the host is part of a panel of judges, whilst the designers have a separate mentor figure who supports them in the workroom. Each week, guest experts are brought in to advise and judge contestants.

In lifestyle experiment and makeover shows, mentors and experts may take an active role, guiding and training participants – especially in shows like *Supernanny* or *Queer Eye* that are built around the experts' personalities. At other times, they may be a presence only the audience see, such as the historians who provide 'the history bit' on *Great British Sewing Bee* and *The Great British Bake Off (GBBO)*, whose role is not to support the contestants but to educate viewers.

The type of personalities recruited for these roles vary from show to show. Sometimes, they are people who have expertise relevant to the programme but are not famous outside their own field, such as Tim Gunn, *Project Runway* mentor (S1-16) who was recruited for his background in fashion education, or Margaret Mountford and Nick Hewer, the aides on early series of the UK *Apprentice* who were chosen for their business backgrounds and connections with Alan Sugar. These people often become celebrities and many have gone on to other media-related projects. Gunn, had his own *PR* spin-off show, *Under the Gunn*, and recently announced a new venture with Amazon, alongside former *PR* host Heidi Klum. Nick Hewer left *The Apprentice* to host daytime quiz *Countdown*. He and Mountford also presented a series of factual BBC shows together, and whilst Mountford left the show to complete a PhD in papyrology, this led to her being offered history presenting roles with the BBC.

Other mentors and judges are household names before they are recruited. The *X Factor* (and later *Got Talent*) judge, Sharon Osbourne, was ostensibly recruited for her expertise in rock management, but that she was fresh from the success of *The Osbournes*, a fly-on-the-wall series about her family, seems unlikely to be a coincidence (see Chapter 5). Various international versions of *The Voice* have attracted high-profile artists who are still having hits as mentors, such as Katy Perry, Pharrell Williams, Kylie Minogue and Rita Ora.

Graduates of reality shows are another popular choice for these roles. Talent shows such as The *X Factor* and *The Voice* have seen various reality alumni, including Jennifer Hudson, Cheryl, Louis Tomlinson, Olly Murs, Nicole Scherzinger and Adam Lambert return as judges, mentors and guest experts. *Project Runway* has occasionally brought back former winners and finalists as guest judges (although sparingly, so as not to dilute its own All-Stars brand based around returnees), and replaced Gunn as series mentor with former winner (and, arguably, the most successful of its graduates) Christian Siriano. *Great British Menu* has an interim judging stage overseen by former contestants, or 'veterans', before chefs meet the 'real' judging panel. *RuPaul's Drag Race* often invites back former contestants to oversee challenges – and the list goes on.

The presence of returning stars as mentors performs several functions. Firstly, they help solidify the brand of the show – seeing old faces is a pleasure for viewers who remember them (and an inducement for newer viewers to check out old seasons), they are a 'wake-up call' to participants, and a reminder of the show's potential to make stars. They may also command a reduced fee, due to 'brand loyalty' to the show that made them famous (Bonner, 2013; Wilson, 2014).

Mentors, judges and experts play a range of useful functions within reality formats, and there are a variety of styles they adopt. The makeover formats of the mid-00s tended to have no-nonsense experts like *Kitchen Nightmares*' Gordon Ramsay, *Supernanny* Jo Frost, and *What Not to Wear*'s Trinny and Susannah, who would dispense their advice in ways that could seem quite cutting, even though it was in the guise of 'tough love' and a concern for the subject's wellbeing (Sender & Sullivan, 2009) – in a process Brenda Weber calls 'salvation through submission', participants had to yield to the will of these experts who know best.

In contrast, there is a breed of gay male mentor that has a very different approach. Gok Wan in *How to Look Good Naked* personified the 'gay best friend' stereotype as he encouraged women to strip off in the name of body confidence; Tim Gunn would regularly cry on *Project Runway* when contestants were sent home, and the *Queer Eye* reboot involves constant expression of emotion from its five mentor/hosts, who not only show emotional investment in the stories and makeovers of their clients but also reveal their own struggles with homophobia, bullying and self-esteem through tearful revelation. This was especially powerful in the first two series, where we saw black 'culture' mentor Karamo bonding with a Trump supporter, and decorating mentor Bobby sharing his painful relationship with religion when working with Christian clients. It became a little more grating by series four when sometimes the performative emotion of the 'fab five' threatened to dominate the storylines rather than the experiences of their clients.

Mentors and experts can even have their own story arcs. For example, in *Strictly Come Dancing*, storylines involving professional dancers span several series. Series stalwart, Anton Du Beke, is characterised as the unlucky professional whose partners are always terrible (although this narrative is not always borne out by the statistics); but in 2015, was paired with newsreader Katie Derham and reached his first final – which the show presented as his equivalent of a happy ending.

HOSTS WITH THE MOST

Many reality shows are held together by one or more presenters. Their role is largely to orientate the audience as to what is happening at any given time, but they also facilitate timekeeping (especially, in timed challenges or in live broadcasts), offer support for contestants and act in a mediator role when required. In some lifestyle experiment programmes, the host is also the participant – as with Richard Ayoade in *Travel Man* and Peter Owen Jones in *Around the World in 80 Faiths*, or the host is also the mentor/expert/judge, as with Laurence Llewellyn Bowen in *Instant Hotel* or RuPaul in *RuPaul's Drag Race*.

Hosts can form a strong part of the brand image. Ryan Seacrest, for example, is synonymous with *American Idol*, Ant and Dec with *Britain's Got Talent* and *I'm a Celebrity...* (UK version), and Tyra Banks with *America's Next Top Model (ANTM)* (even though she was replaced by Rita Ora for series 23, Banks was so heavily associated with the brand that she returned a series later).

Bonner (2011) notes that little attention is paid to presenters of reality shows in academic accounts, yet they can play a key role in framing and controlling the discourse of programmes, as in the case of *Big Brother* evictions, where the presenter has to ensure the show runs to time as well as asking the questions the public (and producers) want answering and providing pastoral support and reorientation into the world outside the house for bewildered evictees.

There are different approaches to using voiceovers and presenters. Studio-based formats (e.g. *The X Factor, Dancing*

With the Stars, Got Talent) rely on one or more presenters to act as the face of the show, linking sections together, describing the action, explaining how to vote (where relevant) and offering support to participants. These shows may also make use of voiceovers – for example, The *X Factor* UK has often used Peter Dickson, also known as 'voiceover man' to provide dramatic introductions to participants and create a sense of theatre.

Observational formats rely more on voiceovers than presenters, to not interrupt the 'natural' feeling of the action. Makeover shows, meanwhile, often roll the expert and presenter function into one. Many reality shows use a combination of presenter and voiceover, and the voiceover may come from the presenter(s) or a third party.

Reality show presenters and voiceover artists are drawn from several different worlds, most commonly:

- professional television presenters, with a track record in hosting similar programmes (e.g. Dermot O'Leary, Emma Willis, Cat Deeley).

- celebrities drawn from the field covered in the programme – modelling, cookery, property, music, athletics, etc. (e.g. Tyra Banks, Piers Taylor, Gordon Ramsay).

- former reality show contestants (e.g. Rylan Clark-Neal, Brian Dowling, Liam Charles).

- comedians (e.g. Terry Crews, Rob Beckett, Jo Brand).

The choice of presenter often depends on the nature of the programme, not only in terms of format but also tone and approach. Comedians are often used for light-hearted entertainment-focused shows (e.g. *All Together Now, ... Got Talent*), or for spin-off shows, which tend to be more anarchic and irreverent than the 'main' show. Comedic and light-entertainment presenters may make a virtue of being 'real' by adding in mistakes and blunders. For example, Claudia Winkleman in *Strictly Come Dancing* often engages in fits of giggles and pratfalls that prove her lack of pretension and emphasise that the broadcast is live.

Writing about double act Mel and Sue, Bonner (2003) notes that they

> *perform ordinariness through a display of apparent incompetence .... Performance in this mode, like an assumed ignorance of the world, operates as another device to diminish distance, making [them] more like us (the viewers). (p. 70)*

Although this was written before they hosted *The Great British Bake Off*, this was clearly evident in how they approached that show, when they would cause havoc for contestants by stealing food, distracting them or dropping things. As my former *GBBO* participant interviewee told me, they also used to swear a lot if a contestant was going through a hard time as a way of subverting the filming because that footage would be unusable! New *GBBO* hosts, Noel Fielding and Sandi Toksvig, have carried on that tradition of a slightly anarchic approach to hosting.

When comedians provide voiceovers for reality shows, they offer a gentle 'ribbing' of participants that adds to the appeal of the programmes – demonstrating self-awareness of the low regard the genre is held in, and mocking its tropes so that the audience do not have to:

> *Now if I know* Love Island, *which I do, there's something ridiculous coming, which there is, that cost a lot of money, which it didn't, cos we're cheap, which we are. (*Love Island Australia *S1 E20)*

Bonner argues that presenters play an important role in establishing the voice of a show:

> *Presenters speak on behalf of programmes as a whole; they are embodiments of the programme's ethos and are permitted to speak as the authority which determines its shape and direction. They do not often do this in the first person singular, preferring the plural. (Bonner, 2003, p. 68)*

However, presenters' control and importance varies according to format (Bonner, 2011). For example, Simon Cowell does not present any of the reality shows he is associated with, yet as executive producer and head judge, he is considered the face and the central authority in these shows. In contrast, it was never in doubt that chat show hosts like Jeremy Kyle and Jerry Springer ruled the roost on the shows they presented, produced and put their names to.

That is not to say that, in formats where a presenter's authority is not necessarily seen as central as an expert or judge's, that they have no power or control. Indeed, they exercise a great deal of authority as the ones who anchor proceedings. In addition, in formats such as talent shows:

> *The presenters mediate between these professional opinions and the tastes and preferences of ordinary voters, usually being encouraging in their comments about contestants and even slightly critical about judges who had become a little blunt in their assessments of professional handicaps. (Bonner, 2011, p. 130)*

They thus prove a very useful tool in establishing the apparent fairness and neutrality in these shows, even if the more cynical viewer might perceive that they are simply playing a role assigned to them in a way that will achieve the desired outcome for the show. For example, backing an 'underdog' contestant to bolster their support after harsh judge criticisms can either be seen as consoling a contestant who has no hope and softening the blow, or, conversely, bolstering the public to vote against the 'mean' judges. It is hard to know, therefore, if the reactions of presenters in these situations are spontaneous and heartfelt, or meticulously planned and specified before broadcast.

HOW AND WHY PEOPLE TAKE PART

Reality television is now a long-established phenomenon, and its impact on participants well-known. As discussed in Chapter 3 this impact is not always positive, and the process of taking part in reality shows and dealing with the response to these programmes can be highly stressful for participants.

Even those who win shows are not guaranteed fame and fortune – the story of reality television is littered with winners who have struggled to sustain careers in the spotlight (see Chapter 5) and prize funds for shows like *Project Runway* and *American Idol* are tied into professional contracts rather than providing cash lump sums to winners. When winners do receive cash, this is not necessarily a huge amount – *Love Island*'s £50,000 prize is split between both parts of a couple, for example. Many shows, particularly observational and social experiment formats, do not offer any form of prize and little, if anything, in the way of financial compensation.

Therefore, unsurprisingly, one of the most common questions people have about reality TV is why on earth people take part in the first place.

It is worth pointing out here that there are a range of different application processes – and in some cases, participants are not explicitly looking to take part in a reality show. Long-established franchises like *Got Talent* and the *The Great British Bake Off* provide a web address for participants to visit if they want to apply, but for one-off and new shows, there are different strategies. Calls for participants are distributed on social media, placed in newspapers, magazines and via reality casting portals like *StarNow*.

However, for programmes with a more specialised focus (such as those involving members of minority communities), production companies often take a more direct approach, contacting community groups and individuals directly, whether via social media, email or visits. My interviewees had different experiences of this scouting process:

> *[I found out] Through Facebook. There was a group I was admin for and the documentary company advertised in a couple of groups I admined. And I thought 'oh, that sounds interesting'. So I read about what they were trying to do and they were trying to educate people on the social side of being trans, so I thought that was something I'd like to get involved with, so I contacted them. (Observational participant)*

> *They were trying to do some investigating on big families and somebody contacted us, wanted to do some research, basically to find out .... They came down for the day with the camera [to shoot test footage] .... They came back to us a couple of times with a few ideas that we said no to and then they said they really liked this interview with [teenage daughter], they'd like to do something with [her] .... We said yeah that would be quite interesting and played with some ideas. (Participants in observational programme)*

They had my number, you know, I'd just get rung
up and asked if I'd speak on this, that or the other
and I did more and more things and I think I'd had
a very intense experience and they saw that I could
do it. (Reality show mentor)

Motivation for taking part in these programmes varies. For several participants, especially from minority communities, a key factor was raising awareness and challenging stereotypes.

When I was doing my activism [previously] I
could only dream of that platform. They gave me
a platform to educate people, albeit in a different
way. I spoke to the others in the documentary and
we've all done it for the same reason. We haven't
done it to get our 15 minutes of fame, we've done
it to make our lives understood and to make every
other trans person out there understood .... There's
a lot of negative press about we trans people and
putting the documentary out there shows we are
just regular people .... this is what we sacrifice and
put on the line to be us, this is what our partners,
friends, family go through .... It's all about
education, we did that documentary to educate.
(Observational participant)

For others, there is the possibility of personal growth and challenge:

In my life I'd really hit a few questions because
I'd had a miscarriage so on a personal level it was
because I saw an opportunity to reflect and get
away from my, everything .... but it was also a
spiritual thing and an intellectual thing. I wanted
to question because I thought that if I rejected
religion altogether and the people who believed in

> *those religions then I was probably as pig-headed as the other way round, so I wanted to question that, challenge it. (Religion-themed social experiment participant)*

Friends and family also play a key part:

> *I did [it] on the advice of a very experienced close friend who is a journalist from the BBC and he encouraged me to do it and I thought well if he's encouraging me to do it then I can trust him. (Social experiment mentor)*

> *I took bakes into work and my work colleagues encouraged me, you really must go onto* Bake Off. *It was Christmas and we were making resolutions about what we were going to do in the coming year and I said I was going to apply. (*The Great British Bake Off *participant)*

The application process for most reality shows has several stages and, alongside warnings about the potential psychological impact (see Chapter 3), these can include application forms, video and in-person auditions, interviews, psychological assessments, group activities, screen tests, social media training (see Chapter 6) and dummy-runs of shows:

> *I got a telephone interview and that was telling me I was onto the next stage. There's a lengthy application form and a telephone interview where they check you've not put anything inaccurate, or downright lies on your application form, and they're testing a little bit of your baking knowledge, and from then on it's about you going to physical auditions where you take along bakes and they do a screen test to make sure you're comfortable in front*

of the camera, and the final auditions, it's basically a cookery school where you were baking with the cameras on you. They bought the cheapest scales and I couldn't work out how to get on with them at all ... and all the time I was chatting away and they must have thought this man is very inept but he would be good on TV! (The Great British Bake Off *participant*)

It was a long process actually. The first, the initial expression of interest, then a form, [on] which you had to make a statement as to why you wanted to get involved, then a further statement, a more in-depth statement. Then they came and interviewed in-house ... and then there was an interview in London as well. So there was quite a lot of process where I had to kind of look and explain why I was going in. (Social experiment participant)

With Sorority Girls, *I filled in an online application, then had a phone call, then I was invited down to a filming day with 50 other girls when there was 13 places to fill. We were literally asked one question on camera (it took about 3 hours to go through everyone) then 30 names were called out and told they were unsuccessful. The remaining girls filmed a scene and 7 more were cut (this made it to episode 1) .... All I knew was a basic outline of the show, and that I had to be female, living in the UK, at university aged between 18–22. For* First Dates, *I literally applied over a year ago! But because the process involves real matchmakers, when they find a match for you they call you and film the same week. (Claudia Wright, participant in two reality shows)*

Whilst some reality shows, such as *First Dates* or *Nailed It!*, change cast every episode and only require a comparatively small time commitment, others involve more significant disruption to participants' lives. Social experiment formats often involve people spending weeks away from home and work. Formats such as *Gogglebox* and *The Great British Bake Off* are filmed alongside people's regular day-to-day commitments, and some more observational formats film aspects of people's work and home lives 'as they happen' (although, despite the naturalised set up, these sometimes involve setting up particular scenes and re-filming sequences, which undermines the idea of them representing natural and spontaneous happenings):

> *The audition process took a couple of months, really, January to March. [Then] they come and film what they call your back story … your real life …. Then from April, filming was every weekend for as long as you were in.* (The Great British Bake Off participant)

> *I think it took eight weeks with a two week break in the middle … sometimes they'd come for like three days in a row and then they would go back for the weekend and come back so it wasn't every single day but when they were down it'd be long days …. A lot of the time they would be here from quite early in the morning to late at night, long hard days …. One of the hardest [things was] you know how you're tired after a long journey, they wanted us to film us getting everything out, making the bed … you just wanted to go to your room and they were asking you all these questions.* (Observational participants)

REALITY SHOW STORIES

In the majority of programmes, a clear narrative arc is established at the start for each participant, although the nature of this differs between shows. It is easier for pre-recorded shows (e.g. most makeover and lifestyle experiment shows) to do this, as they have filmed the whole 'journey' and can construct the narrative retrospectively. It is somewhat harder for shows that are filmed as they happen and/or rely on audience votes (e.g. *Big Brother, I'm a Celebrity*, various talent shows...) as there is some degree of unpredictability here. Even so, through using some pre-recorded material such as auditions and introductory video clips (VTs), these shows usually attempt to create a narrative hook for each participant that demonstrates why they need the intervention of reality TV:

> *I didn't think that I would hit 37 and – unmarried with no kids. Clearly I'm not the best one to make decisions for myself in choosing a partner. (Clare,* Married at First Sight Australia *S1 E1)*

> *I am going to discover what faith I have. I don't know what I believe in. I'm going to be 65 in a couple of weeks and I thought I'd better find out. (Les Dennis,* Pilgrimage, *S2E1)*

One of the most common used words in the reality canon is 'journey'. Shows may take viewers on a journey – for example, learning about a new country or culture, but, more often, the journey is for those who are taking part. Competitive and social experiment formats involve the journeys of several participants, whilst makeovers usually involve one participant at a time. There are also observational and travelogue shows that focus on the journey of one person, who may or may not also narrate the programme (e.g. *The Ganges with Sue Perkins, Extreme Pilgrim*).

All shows have certain parameters to work within – most obviously running time, including advertising breaks – and the timing and structuring of any advertising breaks shapes the narrative significantly. Some will begin an episode with a recap of previous episodes and/or a preview of what is to come in this episode, then they may have another preview before the advert break, a brief recap after the break, and a trailer for the next episode at the end. Add to this the inclusion of previous footage to show a participant's journey or judging deliberations and, in the most extreme cases, there is little room for original content! Advertising breaks also have to be strategically placed – in skill-based shows, for example, they usually break after a challenge and before the judging of that challenge, to give viewers a reason to return, whilst in fly-on-the-wall shows a break will usually come after a dramatic moment such as a fight, a shock or an emotional reaction from a participant.

Most shows have a precise running-order that each episode adheres to, and this is especially the case in formats where the participants change every episode. Keeping to a rigid format helps orient the audience and establishes the regular presenters, narrators and experts as their trusted guides through the process. For example, makeover shows like *Queer Eye* and *Ramsay's Kitchen Nightmares* have a clear standard format that means the same scene will play out at the same time in any given episode. Most of these shows even come with a disclaimer on the credits highlighting that the order of events has been altered, meaning that preserving the format is more important than showing the messy 'reality'.

Shows like these will usually establish the problem – the people and spaces in need of making over, then there will be a mixture of enthusiasm and rebellion as the experts suggest changes, there will be a moment of emotional 'breakthrough' when the clients realise that they are ready to change, then the makeover itself, the reveal, the teething troubles of the clients sticking to the changes, and the end result, which is usually an improvement not only in the appearance of the clients, their homes/businesses, etc., but also a sense of the person having undergone a complete emotional and lifestyle transformation (Raisborough, 2011; Weber, 2009).

For an example of this process in action, let us take a look at a storyline from makeover show *Queer Eye*.

In the first episode of the Netflix reboot, we meet Tom. His daughter nominated him for the show because 'my dad is a hot mess'. Tom himself says: 'I'm just a dumb ol' country boy from Texas … I think I'm unlucky in love because I'm butt ugly. You might make me look a little better, but you can't fix ugly'. His problems are presented as a lack of self-love and self-esteem that has caused him to lose control of his diet, physical appearance, his home, and his relationships (much is made of his three divorces).

When the 'fab five' visit, they immediately identify problems, using humour to pick on aspects of Tom's lifestyle, as when 'fashion expert' Tan France finds a pair of snowflake pyjamas and remarks: 'No-one wants to have sex with you while you're wearing pyjamas like this. I'm beginning to understand why the women are staying away'. The five go around Tom's home noting the problems in its cleanliness and décor, especially highlighting a stained recliner seat they find in the bedroom, and critique Tom's diet, dress sense and grooming in a similar manner.

However, they emphasise throughout that, despite outward appearances, he is an attractive man both physically and in terms of personality, and emphasise the key ethos of this and most makeover shows: 'I really wanna teach Tom that it's OK to love yourself, to have a relationship with yourself' (Jonathan).

A key moment of transformation is when they take Tom's stained recliner chair to landfill, and Karamo says 'Everything that chair symbolised, everything that that was, sitting in your house, not going out in the world, feeling alone, that's where it's gone, it's in the trash now, brand new you'. Part of the physical makeover they complete on Tom's home involves buying two new chairs for him and his 'lady friend' and decorating expert Bobby says that the physical act of buying an extra chair represents a psychological change Tom needs to make: 'if you open your heart and your mind, knowing that there's going to be somebody else for it, it'll happen'.

By the end of the week, naturally, Tom's home is remodelled and he has undergone a makeover in terms of grooming and style, but the emphasis of the show is that it is not only the techniques used to improve the physical self that are important, it is the relationship the client has built with the mentors and the inner journey he has been on in surrendering to the makeover and accepting change that make the difference.

The makeover format dictates that change is inevitable: 'seeing Tom at the end of the week was such juxtaposition from when we first met him. He was all laughs and all smiles but you could tell deep down something was going on' (Tan). Tom's journey finally completes by inviting his ex-wife, Abby, over to his house and her excitement at the end result, with the implication that Tom has now found the answer to his self-esteem and relationship problems.

WOW MOMENTS

One of the most common techniques in reality TV storytelling is the 'wow moment', or what Laura Grindstaff (1997) terms 'the money shot' – the moment where emotion and the 'real' are laid bare. These are the moments that make audiences stop in their tracks, and can be found in pretty much all genres of reality television, from the moment the judges spin their chairs on *The Voice* to see the surprise owner of an unusual singing voice, to the heartrending wow moment of observational series *Educating Yorkshire* in which teenage stuttering Musharaf was revealed to be able to speak eloquently whilst listening to music. The Susan Boyle moment this chapter led with is perhaps the epitome of all of these!

For many shows, the wow moment comes at particular predictable points: knowing which contestant is eliminated on a voting show; the initial reveal of a made over person, object or property in makeover shows – although the smart makeover shows will have several wows dropped in: the wow of the before; the wows of different parties when the makeovers are revealed; and maybe some revelatory wows about trauma, disaster or other life circumstance that is revealed in confession.

Korean show *Hidden Singer* has the premise of a panel of judges trying to predict which of six secret voices is a famous singer on sound alone. The wow moments come when they discover the ordinary people passing themselves off as the celebrity, particularly if these contestants are unusual in appearance, gender or age. There is the wow moment when it is revealed which door the real singer is behind and in some episodes, a wow moment when another popular singer has been revealed as one of those offering their voice.

RuPaul's Drag Race offers wow moments of the more spectacular variety-amazing jokes, jaw-dropping runway outfits, athletic lip syncs and of the more revelatory variety, where participants reveal tragic awe-inspiring stories from their personal life.

In many cases, the wow moment is the climax of the narrative – but that does neither necessarily mean the climax of a series or even an individual show, nor does it necessarily mean the end of a participant's journey – it simply marks the climax of one strand of the story and the marker point for which a new narrative can be written, a new direction can be taken or a new challenge can be introduced.

This is especially the case in series that follow participants through multiple episodes – we witness their journey across several different episodes and the wow moment or moments can come at different points to help establish whereabouts and the journey they are. For example, a show like *The Choir* will use a wow moment to tell others how beautiful somebody's voice is when they audition, but will also give us wows as we with learn the true story behind that participant's life- often one of struggle. There are wow moments where perhaps they rebel or look certain to drop out. And, the biggest wows of all are when they perform and overcome their demons.

EXITS AND ENDINGS

Not only do reality television narratives have a start that establishes the aims, and a middle full of key moments, they, of course, have endings. The nature of these endpoints varies slightly –some programmes tell one story per episode. In programmes that involve lifestyle experiments, the endpoint is usually the final episode.

However, in competitive formats, there are multiple endpoints as each participant is dismissed. And whilst producers may be able to anticipate storylines and actions, they cannot entirely anticipate what participants will do – and how viewers will vote in programmes where they have a say.

Despite this, the framing of the end of journeys is usually one that brings a satisfying conclusion – most commonly when a participant has achieved the goal established for them at the start of the programme/series. The confirmation of them having reached this goal is usually given in a confessional interview. Even in competitive formats where they are eliminated before the end, the contestant usually agrees with the exit from the show and the fact that they had come to the end of their natural journey.

Sometimes, they show a degree of sadness and disappointment that they had not progressed as far as they wanted to more fully achieve their goals. In such cases, the audience may be invited to question the validity of what is shown – that is, perhaps, we are privy to knowledge about them that they are not privy to themselves and we understand that the ousting is deserved. Other times, this sense of a journey not yet complete leads to an opportunity for the participant to return in a reunion format through which they can finally achieve a level of validation.

When a villain comes to the end of their narrative, this is usually a sign of justified comeuppance. It might come through them being evicted for breaking a rule, or through the standard elimination process whereby the judge or audience opt to send them home at a particular point, usually once they have proved their worth in entertainment value.

Whether or not participants accept their role as the villain varies significantly. A repentant villain might own up to their bad behaviour and accept their ousting's justifiable punishment. However, they may challenge this narrative and suggest they should not have been axed. This is not necessarily a problem for programme makers. It can be spun that their refusal to accept their demise reinforces that they had not sufficiently learned the appropriate lessons of reality television by performing as a good citizen and accepting the show's outcomes.

In some reality shows, the likelihood of a participant being seen to accept their journey is less important than others. *The Apprentice* emphasises participant bravado, bluster and swagger – whilst undermining that through a seemingly incompetent performance in series of often unfeasibly difficult and artificial task-based scenarios. Its participants will often give an exit interview bemoaning their exit. But viewers are rarely expected to side with the evicted candidate, instead we are meant to see their blustering exit interview as proof of their incompetence and self-delusion.

BREAKING THE RULES

As we saw with the Susan Boyle example that opened this chapter, occasionally reality shows will deliberately subvert their established norms, and thus, our expectations. As well as challenging the stereotypes they have created, as in Boyle's case, shows occasionally break their own rules. For example, in skill and talent shows which have a usual 'one out per week, one winner per series' structure, judges might break the format by eliminating more than one participant, eliminating no-one, or crowning more than one winner. By breaking the rules, these shows attempt to reinforce how 'real' they are – making out that justice will prevail, and fairness is more important than a strict template.

Yet, it is hard to argue that this process *is* always 'fair' – and in some cases, audiences are cynical as to the motives for these changes, arguing that there have been previous episodes where such a rule break should have been implemented but was not, and that sometimes the justification for breaking the rules is really an attempt by producers to manipulate the series and keep in those who 'make good TV' rather than those who are the most successful at the challenges.

It is important to only break formats sparingly as audiences often react negatively to such choices. Even though audience comments after finales often speak of wishing they could give the prize to one or more of the finalists, arguing that their preferred finalist was robbed and so on, this seems to be part of the effective viewing experience, because when two winners *are* crowned in a series there is often an accusation of 'copout' or producer manipulation.

In the 2019 series of *RuPaul's Drag Race All Stars*, the win was given to both Trinity the Tuck and Monet XChange. The editing of the show did not show the two queens receiving the accolade together or posing for any victory footage together, and fans speculated that a two winner ending had not been part of the plan for the show until much later in the day, and it was a last-minute change to please fans that, instead, had the opposite effect (Damshenas, 2019).

Makeover formats also occasionally stray from their usual template. Occasionally, they feature a client so resistant that they never fully change, or they pull the plug on filming partway through. In these instances, the narrative is spun so that 'if only' they had listened to the experts, things would have improved, but now they would not. This kind of narrative reinforces the aims of these programmes to be life-changing and the power of the experts to do so – as long as a client is willing to submit to their ideas. It also acts as a claim to the shows' authenticity – if they film an unsuccessful make-over attempt, it 'proves' their reality and the idea that 'anything can happen', even if the majority of episodes and their rigid narrative structure suggests otherwise.

A key component of many makeover shows is revisiting the clients sometime after filming has stopped. Usually, we see the continued impact of the makeover, proving the transformation is 'real' and not just for television. However, on occasion, we see the client reverting to 'old ways', or being tempted to do so. This is the makeover show's equivalent of a film with an ending that sets up a sequel – because most makeover formats, once they have a few series under their belt, have a 'revisit' strand.

In revisits, the experts return to their clients some months or years later, and find either the same problems, or new ones, to fix. The revisit is not only a nice hook for the audience to see 'what happened next' but also a budget-friendly approach to making television as often these episodes are full of repeated content from the initial visit, interspersed with a smattering of new scenes.

IS IT ALL FAKE?

The limitations of format described above allow for little deviation – which might lead us to speculate on how 'real' these shows are. Some shows are very open about creating particular scenarios for TV rather than just allowing them to occur naturally, and often part of the fun for audiences is speculating on how contrived these things are, and what has and has not been included in the edit. Even shows that take a fly-on-the-wall approach, with the aim to capture life 'as it happens' involve processes of editing and selecting footage from weeks of filming to fill short television slots.

But what is involved in this process, do participants have any say in what is, and is not, included, and how do they feel about the final edit?

Those who have taken part in observational formats following them as individuals or families often expressed a greater amount of control over what was filmed and included than other participants:

> *They came up with some suggestions and we*
> *knocked them down, they came up with some*
> *better suggestions. They came up with a proposal*

> *that felt good enough …. they came up with release*
> *forms and so on that we weren't happy with and*
> *so we sent them back and they came up with better*
> *ones … [we] didn't expect that they would let us*
> *see what went on, but they did, they took a DVD*
> *down and we were allowed to watch it and give*
> *comments about it, what we thought and they*
> *made changes we asked them to. (Observational*
> *participants)*

One observational participant discussed how she engaged in regular dialogue with the production team about what would be filmed – they came every so often to track her progress over time; they would come to film if she was doing something interesting and sometimes they required her to come to their studio for close-up filming. Most things they filmed were part of her daily life, although one specific situation was created for television. She is a UK resident, but the film also showed her travelling to the USA, which was something they arranged for her:

> *I went to LA for speech therapy. They tried to get*
> *into my sessions in the UK but the NHS didn't want*
> *them to film it. So they gave me the opportunity to*
> *go abroad.*

In these instances, there is greater agency afforded for two key reasons – firstly, as the sole subjects of their programmes, if they refused to film then there would not be a programme! And secondly, the first participants quoted are a family whose children were filmed, and the second is a trans woman whose transitioning process was closely examined in detail, including medical and family aspects (her children were also filmed). The perceived sensitivity of these subjects no doubt played a key role in the way producers exercised duty of care.

Other programmes vary in their filming and editing approaches. In *The Great British Bake Off*, for instance, participants have to complete the challenges in the time and manner shown to viewers, which my interviewee laughingly called a 'nightmare':

> *And people say it's not real is it? Yeah, it's*
> *absolutely real. Because at home you're used to*
> *doing a bit of something, then pottering ... You*
> *don't have that luxury, you have to concentrate for*
> *an hour, two hours, three, four ... [It's] an exercise*
> *in discipline... There was very little re-recording*
> *.... The stuff in the tent was quite spontaneous ....*
> *There's a bit of editing I think in terms of the judges*
> *reactions, and they'll film the announcements again,*
> *so they'll film Sue saying you've got an hour left*
> *when you've only got ten minutes.*

Social experiment and observational formats tend to combine fly-on-the-wall techniques where everything is filmed with specifically set-up scenes:

> *EVERYTHING on SG was staged. For example,*
> *when we all ran into a room to find a surprise,*
> *we had to refilm it three times so the camera men*
> *could get different angles but still look 'shocked'.*
> *The producers make you say certain things or kind*
> *of put words in your mouth. I thought filming*
> *was hilarious, but the writer of the show was a*
> *really stiff American sorority house woman so she*
> *made the edited version- the one shown- quite dull*
> *compared to what I thought it was going to be.*
> *(Claudia, Sorority Girls – a social experiment in*
> *which an American sorority was created in a British*
> *university)*

They said they didn't want to organise anything, they didn't want to set anything up, they wanted to just film it naturally and then all of the way through they set it up! Can we do that again, and again, can you do it over here? They had to get it with the right angles, didn't they, to make it look good. (Observational participant)

There were several things set up that they did use. I mean they asked [teenager] several times not to smile and sort of look wistfully out of the window and so on which is not the girl she is ... when they put on sad music and pull the camera away. It makes it look, oh, poor girl. I had one email saying I want to give you a hug and I had to laugh because when it pulls away and there's the sad music and the clouds and everything, they had to walk backwards with the camera and were stepping in the muddy puddles, and we had a photographer there that day as well and he was like, taking pictures and slipped down into a puddle... So we were all laughing and laughing and we had to stop. (Observational participants)

They were there pretty much seventeen hours a day ... you didn't know what they were going to film, they were filming different things each day, so I think what they did was filmed through the different sections of the day at various different points and then they swapped that over, and then they would focus in on one person and that's the person they'd film, where the story was going. So for me, for example, there was a fairly significant period where I wasn't filmed that much. (Social experiment participant)

The format you see is exactly what it's like. There's about 2/3 set-up dates going on at once, and all the rest are just background people to fill the seats. Hidden camera too so it really feels like a normal date! ... It's set up by actual matchmakers so it is about finding love. Also, the guy I was set up with, I actually matched with him on Tinder months ago but we just never spoke so they did something right! (Claudia, First Dates)

When it comes to how they feel about their portrayal, however, participants have very mixed feelings. The genre of reality show memoirs is full of contestants angered by unfair treatment. My own interviewees had quite dramatically different experiences of how they perceived their edits:

Things I did say were manipulated ... when you've got somebody asking questions and you take the questions out and put a voiceover in then you get a very different answer. And the questions were very leading, which is why after about three weeks they stopped filming me because I'd sussed out what they were doing and wouldn't answer them ... I think they did a number on everybody. (Social experiment participant)

It's interesting because I think people expect that you've been involved in the editing or have seen an early [version], but you haven't, you're seeing it at the same point as everybody else ... They were really, really kind and there was one week I think I said something inappropriate about work and I said can you check that's not in, and they said don't worry, we wouldn't put that in anyway. And I think they don't want to put anything in that's

*going to ... create too much drama. The
drama is in the series [format], they don't
want to make it look like we're all backstabbing
and bickering, which we weren't. (*GBBO
participant)

*I was made out to be eliminated for having
'explicit' photos on FB, which was totally false.
They already know who they want the winners to
be before we even start filming- so I knew they just
had to invent a reason for me to go. I hated the way
I left. I actually ripped my microphone off and left
the room because I was angry at how they were
making me look on TV. The producers convinced
me (an hour later!) to come back in the room to
finish filming but I still got cut. I think I dropped
the F bomb, which I probably shouldn't have!
(Claudia,* Sorority Girls)

*[I was told] That it was going to be unbiased, and
[presenter] who did the interviews was just clearly
very biased, clearly she had a real, she was like a
dog with a bone in the interviewing and when I
saw the programme with her whole manner with
other people she interviewed was entirely different
from the way she went at me ... I mean the woman
didn't want the answer I gave her and she just kept
asking the question until I said what she wanted
me to say and it was a pretty appalling experience.
(Studio interview participant)*

One of my interviewees spoke about how, for her, dealing
with a miscarriage had been a huge part of her journey, and
a motivation for her participation, yet this was not featured
in the final edit:

*For them not to have mentioned it they took out
probably about 80% of what I was talking about
and it made me so angry, because one of the
problems I had was that people don't talk about
it and then they did the same thing. They silenced
it, they said right, it's unimportant and [they
removed] so much more personal stuff in order to
present me as what they wanted to present me as,
which I thought was really stupid actually ....
I think the thing was, the shocking thing was,
I trusted them because I was filming 17-hour
days, because the process of application had
been so long and because of the environment we
were in which it's imperative that you trust.
I really did trust that they were going to
make an intelligent, insightful programme
that would help people. (Social experiment
participant)*

As to whether or not people regretted their experiences,
though, even some of those who were most critical claimed to
have benefited in some way:

*It was extreme, actually, but at the same time when
I look back on it, it was actually a really special
time because it was a really different world, even
though the television crew were there.
(LE participant)*

I'm not exactly happy with the documentary
perfectly, *but I'm happy with the results so I'm glad
we did it. (Observational participant)*

*I don't regret anything. I love reality TV and I loved
my opportunity to appear on it. (Claudia)*

CONCLUSION

Whilst it is impossible to say that every reality show is formulaic and predictable, there are certainly many instances where this is the case. However, it can be easy to forget that the people on camera are not all there for the same reason, or to tell the same story. Sometimes, they get from it what they expected, at other times less so.

One of the things reality participants are most accused of wanting is celebrity – and that is where we will turn our attention next.

5

REALITY TV AND CELEBRITY

In 2009, Jade Goody, a 27-year old mother of two and former dental nurse, died of cervical cancer. Her illness, death and funeral made the front pages of magazines and newspapers in the UK and made headlines around the world. Goody, perhaps more than anyone else, epitomised the 2000s model of the 'reality star'. She became famous as a participant in the third series of *Big Brother* UK in 2002 and learned of her cancer diagnosis in 2008 whilst taking part in *Big Boss*, the Indian iteration of the franchise, in an unfortunate narrative twist.

Initially, Goody had seemed an unlikely candidate for sustained fame. An early public vote for the least favourite housemate saw Goody receive many more votes than her closest competitor, Lynne Moncrieffe. However, when fellow competitors voted Goody to remain over Moncrieffe, her life – and, arguably, the world of reality celebrity – was changed forever.

Goody's journey in the *Big Brother* house saw her regularly escape nomination for eviction until the show's final, in which she finished fourth of four. She was shown to be the least popular housemate in both of the public votes she faced;

however by the time of her funeral, she was mourned by many fans. So, what happened in between her reality 'birth' and her untimely death?

Goody had a strongly identifiable persona. Whether exaggerated or not, during *Big Brother* she became notable for her naivete and ignorance, with her questions over whether 'East Angular' was a country or Rio de Janeiro a person becoming catchphrases that were routinely repeated both by her fans and detractors. Jade quickly became a 'Marmite' personality – loved and hated in equal measure. With a more distinctive personality than many of her fellow competitors, she was in demand after the show finished and appeared regularly across TV, magazines and the press.

Within the space of a few years, she starred in several further reality shows, some, like *Big Brother*, were competitive formats (e.g. *Back to Reality, Stars in Their Eyes)* and others were centred on her life (e.g. *Just Jade, Jade's PA*), and even in her illness and death (e.g. *Jade's Progress, Jade: A Year Without Her*). During the six-and-a-half years between *Big Brother* and her death, she had appeared on 16 different reality shows and dozens of talk shows, panel shows and entertainment shows. She released several workout DVDs, an autobiography, a fragrance and was rarely out of celebrity magazines and the tabloid press. She had two children with fellow reality star, Jeff Brazier, broke up with Brazier, and dated and married Jack Tweed. Tweed and her mother, Jackiey Budden, also became celebrities through their connections to Jade.

What makes Jade especially interesting is not only her trajectory from ordinary young woman to ubiquitous celebrity to tragic heroine but also that there were points in her career in the spotlight where she became seen as a villain. The years immediately following her *Big Brother* appearance saw her move from someone who was largely a figure of fun or disdain to someone who was generally well-liked – redeeming herself by playing the role of 'just Jade' wherever she was featured, and setting a prototype for many reality stars to follow, including fellow Essex-based stars, Joey Essex and Gemma Collins, who found fame through *The Only Way is Essex (TOWIE)* – indeed, without Jade, there probably would not even be *TOWIE*. However, Jade's image took a hit in 2007 when she, along with Jack and Jackiey, took part in *Celebrity Big Brother (CBB)* 5. Whilst the celebrity format had been running for a few series, this marked the first (and only – reunion formats such as *Ultimate Big Brother* excepted) time a contestant from the 'civilian' show had also been included in the celebrity variant.

Goody's time in the house was marked by controversy from the beginning, as the rest of the housemates took part in a task that saw Goody and family being presented as royalty and other members of the cast having to take the roles of their servants. This twist saw both filmmaker Ken Russell and singer Donny Tourette walk out of the show in protest.

As the series developed, Jade, Jack and fellow contestants, Jo O'Meara and Danielle Lloyd, got into a rivalry with Bollywood actress, Shilpa Shetty, and audiences complained to Channel 4 and Ofcom about the trio bullying her and using racist insults (Rahman, 2008). Jade was unceremoniously evicted through the back door with no eviction crowd and faced an uncomfortable interview with host, Davina McCall.

She then made many public apologies and her appearance in *Big Boss* the following year was both an attention-seeking move on behalf of the show, capitalising on the controversy, and an attempt at image rehabilitation from Goody. Prior to exiting the Celebrity Big Brother house, Jade told fellow housemates 'I said, it [*Big Brother*] was the beginning of my career and the end of it', which it was, in the most unforeseeable of ways.

Media coverage of her in death, much as in life, was full of mixed views and much hand-wringing from columnists who worried not only about her as an undesirable form of celebrity but also wanted to celebrate her connection to the public (Holmes, 2009; Tyler & Bennett, 2009). Raisborough, Frith and Klein (2013) note that in press coverage, 'motherhood played a crucial role redeeming Jade's character – albeit unevenly' (p. 258) as a way of at least partially redeeming from being portrayed solely as a typical 'celebrity chav' (Tyler & Bennett, 2009) classless, taste-free attention-seeker.

Goody was neither the first breakout reality star, nor even the most famous – yet, arguably more than any other, she epitomises the complex relationship between reality television and fame, and the way in which public opinion is a precarious business. As I write, the tenth anniversary of her death has just passed, accompanied by retrospectives about her career and updates on the supporting cast of her life. Jeff Brazier has given confessional interviews discussing his new role as a life-coach and providing updates on their sons' wellbeing, sharing the ways the family memorialised Jade such as hosting charity events, and his sense of duty to keep her memory alive. Jack Tweed and Jackiey Budden have both provided mediated performances of grief on TV interviews and being photographed at her graveside. Even in death, the Jade Goody reality show continues.

FROM 'ORDINARY' TO 'CELEBRITY'

Globally, reality television has made stars of hundreds – even thousands – of people. This is not particularly a recent phenomenon (the likes of comedians Lenny Henry and Victoria Wood got their big break on 1970s talent show *New Faces*, for instance) but the sheer number of reality shows in the last

20 years have meant that there are far more reality-grown celebrities than in previous decades, and therefore it might seem as if it is a relatively new route to fame.

Most reality celebrities have had their brief 15 minutes of fame and then faded away, but others have managed to sustain long post-reality careers, including model, Winnie Harlow, (*America's Next Top Model*), presenters, Ben Fogle (*Castaway*) and Alison Hammond (*Big Brother UK*), singers, Jennifer Hudson (*American Idol*) and Nicole Scherzinger (*Popstars*), and actors, Jessie Buckley (*I'd Do Anything*) and Lucy Hale (*American Junior*). Others, too, have made being a reality star their career, moving from show to show, such as Gemma Collins, Bethenny Frankel, Heidi and Spencer Pratt and Courtney Act. Even some of our biggest contemporary stars have had a brush with reality television in the past: Beyoncé, Britney Spears and Justin Timberlake all took part in *Star Search*; Emma Stone competed in *In Search of The Partridge Family*; Jon Hamm was a participant on *The Big Date*.

Whilst the broad category 'celebrity' can encompass as diverse a set of personalities as, say, The Queen, Sylvester Stallone and Kylie Jenner, we do not afford all celebrities the same status and value – and reality stars are often seen as possessing lower value than their counterparts. Chris Rojek (2001) argues that one way to understand this is to think of celebrities according to three categories: achieved (famous for a skill or talent), ascribed (famous through lineage) or attributed (famous for being famous).

These are only a broad outline, and many celebrities fall somewhere between categories: actors with famous relatives such as Miley Cyrus or Elizabeth Olsen could be considered 'ascribed' celebrities, famous through association with relatives who hit the big time first (Billy-Ray Cyrus, Mary-Kate and Ashley Olsen), but it would be hard to deny that they also have talent that has helped sustain their careers, so they could equally be thought of as 'achieved'. The same is true when we think of reality stars: Adam Lambert and Carrie Underwood may have a form of 'attributed' fame from *American Idol*, but, again, they also have talent. To have sustained successful careers in the music industry for many years might, again, position them in the 'achieved' category.

In Rojek's discussion of 'attributed' celebrity, he identifies two key sub-categories of attributed star: the 'celeactor' – a fictional character, often satirical in nature, who acts as a celebrity; and the 'celetoid', someone who becomes famous through their newsworthiness and whose moment in the spotlight is brief.

Whilst celeactors are perhaps less pertinent to a discussion of reality TV fame than celetoids, there are intersections between the two. Most obviously, there are fictional characters in mockumentary programming such as Alan Partridge, David Brent and Michael Scott, who function as 'celebrities'. But there are also some reality performers who blur the lines between playing 'themselves' and playing a character. Irish twins John and Edward Grimes, who are better known as Jedward, might fit here. Originally entering the UK *X Factor* as 'John and Edward', their name was soon shortened to the portmanteau 'Jedward', which became their branding – they maintained their fame through several subsequent reality show appearances and events like Eurovision, but their fame is not built on any knowledge of the real 'John' and 'Edward' but on the 'Jedward' package. There are also animal reality stars, that blur the lines between character and 'real' persona such as Pudsey the dog, who won *Britain's Got Talent* with owner Ashley and appeared as a 'fictionalised' version of himself in his own feature film.

More recently, British reality star, Gemma Collins (who rose to fame in *The Only Way is Essex* in 2011, but has a portfolio of over 20 reality show appearances under her belt), has spoken of having two sides to her persona, 'the real' Gemma Collins, and alter-ego, 'The GC':

> *The GC is a bit of a brand. Obviously there's me, and then the GC. But when the GC's gone, people miss her, they go 'where's the GC'? ... [She is] very outrageous, very 'out there', she doesn't care what she does or what she says, she's very near the mark ... She's almost saying what people want to say but haven't got the guts to say it ... I mean yeah, I am out there as well, but Gemma prefers to be with her family ... doing the shop, cooking dinner. (Gemma Collins on* Good Morning Britain, *2019)*

The idea of performing a character is not confined to reality contestants – British TV host, Lorraine Kelly, recently hit the news for claiming on her tax returns that 'Lorraine Kelly' was a character she plays on television rather than her authentic self!

Collins' attempt to separate her 'real' persona from the 'GC' brand is fascinating. Her whole brand image has been based on reality television – including her very public love life – and her move to separate her identities in two causes us to reflect on her previous performances on television and in confessional interviews – at which points did we see Gemma, and at which GC? Where does one end and the other begin? And as 'the GC' was largely a nickname conferred on Collins by audiences and the media, who created the GC in the first place? And given she was promoting her book *The GC: How to Be a Diva*, to what extent was her attempt to separate the two identities merely a publicity stunt?

This example connects to two key ideas in celebrity studies. Firstly, there is the idea of the 'star image'. Richard Dyer (1979, 1986) has argued that a celebrity's image is not fixed to one moment or site of fame but is 'intertextual', built through appearances and representations in a range of places. The construction of a star image does not only come from the star themselves, but is also a complex process involving 'cultural intermediaries' (Rojek's term for the various people that are involved in building star careers, such as publicists and agents), audiences and the media. He argues that part of the fascination with stars is about speculating which parts of this image are the 'real' person.

This links to our second key idea. In *The Presentation of Self in Everyday Life* (1959), Erving Goffman argues that we have two sides to our self-presentation – the 'front stage' – our public-facing self, and the 'back-stage' – the parts of ourselves that we hide. Celebrity culture – especially the role of gossip, confessional interviews and social media – is all about speculating on the 'back stage' lives of stars, and to what extent these match up with their 'front stage' personae – in other words, how 'real' their image is.

Writers like Graeme Turner (2004, 2010) and Laura Grindstaff (2012) have noted that reality stars take this idea of the 'real' and, rather than demonstrating the mystique of Hollywood legends, make their openness and ordinariness a virtue. Turner (2006) calls the move towards 'ordinary celebrity' represented by reality stars the 'demotic turn' rather than 'democratic' because whilst the broadening of the celebrity category to include ordinary people takes in ideas of the everyday and 'normal', it does not mean that it makes the entire fame process democratic. Not everyone can be a celebrity, and not all celebrities have the same power or status.

Of the many thousands of people who have come through the reality genre, only a select few have managed to make a full-time career of being celebrities. As Turner (2014) notes:

> *Although the 'ordinary person' can use* Big Brother
> *to take a shot at fame, something that was unlikely*

> *to be available to them through any other means,*
> *they are still at the mercy of the system that creates*
> *them and in which they have a very limited*
> *future. (p. 59)*

The creation of celebrities through reality television is an enterprise involving several parties – the reality stars themselves, and those involved in producing the shows, as well as audiences, agents, managers and others within the wider media and entertainment industries. But how does this process work? What makes an Adam Lambert, Ben Fogle, Rylan Clark-Neal or Carrie Underwood stand out from the pack and able to move on from their reality star roots? And even if the answer is 'talent', how does that account for the continued fame of the likes of Katie Hopkins or Bethenny Frankel? It is not always clear cut. Turner argues that:

> *the discourses that construct celebrity are*
> *contradictory. According to them, celebrity is*
> *deserved or totally arbitrary: the recognition of*
> *natural talent or just blind good luck. (Turner,*
> *2004, p. 60)*

Richard Dyer (1986) argues that celebrities are 'intertextual', by which he means that they are not confined to a single site of fame. Celebrities do not only make music, act, play sport or model clothes, but are also visible in newspapers, magazines, social media, chat shows and advertising– and the same is true for reality stars. There is a whole industry underpinning the world of reality celebrity, and those whom the industry anoints as stars through giving them publicity are more likely to achieve fame. Turner notes that this process has a cynical element to it:

> *Casting ordinary people into game shows, docu-*
> *soaps and reality TV programming enables*

> *television producers to 'grow their own' celebrities*
> *and to control how they are marketed before,*
> *during and after production. (Turner, 2010, p. 13)*

Whilst only certain personalities are made into stars this way, we can clearly see this process at work in several high-profile examples. Think of the BBC's adoption of *The Great British Bake Off* winner Nadiya Hussain, turning her very quickly into a TV presenter with several cookery shows, travel documentaries and even a film about anxiety.

Even where people do have fame as at least part of their motivation for taking part in reality shows, they may have different expectations of what this fame may entail, or of what they hope it will do for them. The goal may simply be gaining a larger following on social media, and perhaps being able to monetise that social media account through advertising and promotions (see Chapter 6). For others, it may be continuing working in the fields they have already gained some experience in, but with a bigger publicity base. This is particularly the case for entertainers and singers who take part in talent competitions in the hope to expand their audience on the back of it. For many, this has led to modest success; for a few, it has led to global superstardom.

The size and nature of reality show fame can be highly unpredictable. Participants in shows that have been running for some time may have some understanding of the viewing figures, audience response and potential opportunities they are likely to receive, but viewers are fickle, ratings decline and participants cannot entirely anticipate how they will be received.

People starring in new shows take a leap into the dark as to whether or not it will be popular, how they will be portrayed and what impact it might have on their lives. Early reality stars on fledgling formats often became household names by virtue of their scarcity. Participants in the long-running *Up* series, for example, remark in many episodes on their surprise at being recognised and having people often want to talk to them about their fame (Kilborn, 2010). Likewise, newsworthy people who have turned to reality and factual programming, such as the Walton sextuplet family, have achieved a level of public recognition that may or may not have been their intention.

Even in the first wave of millennial reality television, there was a sense of naïveté on behalf of some of the participants as to the public interest in these shows. Participants in *Castaway 2000* and early *Big Brother* series expressed surprise and bewilderment about public interest in them (Ritchie, 2000). *Castaway* participants were particularly critical of public interest as it led to journalists and members of the public staging invasions on to Taransay, the island they were living on for their social experiment, jettisoning the 'authenticity' of their experience (McCrum, 2000).

Whatever the motivation of participants, whether they expect to become famous, or what they expect that fame to entail, they cannot usually predict what the outcome of a reality show appearance will be. As we have previously seen, participants have little to no control over where they receive a heroic or villainous edit, whether they will be a main player in the show's narrative or a background figure. In a competitive format, they may well be facing people with equal levels of charisma, skill and talent and find it harder than imagined to stand out against the crowd.

Reality stars do not know how audiences will respond to the portrayals of them. People who originally went on a programme primarily for the challenge/experience or to raise awareness (e.g. of a health problem or minority identity) may suddenly find that they have become overnight sensations, recognisable to millions. Conversely, someone who enters a reality show expecting to become a household name may leave as obscure as they were before.

WHAT MAKES A GOOD REALITY CELEBRITY?

The market is so saturated with reality stars now that it is impossible for all of them to make a big impact, and even harder to sustain that fame beyond the show's run. What then might be the determining factors as to whether or not somebody can develop a celebrity career on the back of reality television?

We might imagine that one important factor is novelty. A participant who brings something new or unexpected to the television audience can often make a big impact. The novelty may come from a series being new, unexpected and hitting a chord with an audience, or it may be that, even in a long-established series, a participant offers something predecessors have not.

Think, for example, of Nadia Almada, the winner of *Big Brother* UK series 5 and the first high-profile transgender contestant in that show – or any comparative franchise – in the UK. Her trans status alone did not cement her popularity; but coupled with her quirky sense of humour and her lack of self-belief, she quickly became an endearing figure who shot to fame, receiving magazine covers and even recording her own song after participation. Novelty, along with innate attributes of her personality, catapulted her to victory and short-term fame, but this fame was not sustained with a long media career and when she re-entered the *Big Brother* house for *Ultimate Big Brother*, her experience was altogether different (Lovelock, 2016).

Novelty alone also does not explain why some become famous and others do not. Consider, for example, Rylan

Clark-Neal. A participant on the 2012 UK *X Factor*, Clark-Neal was clearly intended as a lightweight, comedic performer who offered a humour and camp sensibility that played well into the early stages of the competition that rely as much on character building as on performance. He also brought some fun into the early stages of the live shows before the show allegedly starts to focus on serious singers. This was not particularly new-many performers like him had previously come and gone – perhaps, sustaining a short-lived career as novelty celebrities, but often returning to obscurity or semi-obscurity shortly afterwards. He was not even the most noteworthy of the show's comedic contestants.

However, a combination of his warm but eccentric personality, coupled with a very successful stint in the *Celebrity Big Brother* house immediately following his *X Factor* appearance, cemented his star image as fitting into trajectory of camp male TV personalities that includes the likes of Graham Norton and Alan Carr.

Following his *Celebrity Big Brother* win, Clark-Neal quickly became a key television fixture, balancing appearances on further reality shows, including Celebrity *MasterChef*, with guest presenting stints on a whole range of TV programmes. He then took over the lead presenter role on *Big Brother* spin-off, *Big Brother*'s *Bit on the Side*. This led to several further presenting gigs on television and radio, both as a guest and regular host. In 2019, he was announced as both the host of a new makeover show, *You are What You Wear*, and the co-host of *Strictly Come Dancing* spin-off *It Takes Two*. This is a major TV role, previously occupied by Claudia Winkleman, who went on to front several BBC shows, including the main *Strictly Come Dancing* broadcasts; and Zoe Ball, who took over Radio 2's flagship breakfast show in 2019 (both Winkleman and Ball also made the 2019 list of highest-paid BBC Talent).

Let us also consider two other interesting examples from British television. In 2000, British television was dominated by two big reality franchises: *Big Brother* and *Castaway*. Both became media phenomena as we have previously discussed and catapulted their participants to a level of fame. The winner of *Big Brother*, Craig Phillips, has maintained a public profile ever since his victory, yet he has largely featured in the outskirts of fame, as a Do-It-Yourself (DIY) expert on daytime television. In comparison, Ben Fogle, one of the *Castaway* participants has sustained a long career as a presenter of mainstream factual programming (in particular, nature and adventuring documentaries) for several mainstream UK broadcasters. Fogle is also the only member of the *Castaway* cast to have maintained a high public profile.

There may be any number of reasons why Fogle's career has been more successful in terms of his level of fame than Phillips. He is, perhaps, more naturally gifted as a television performer, but there may be other factors at work. Characterised throughout his time in *Castaway* in the media as 'Posh Ben', he has used his affable persona to his advantage. In a media that has long valued received pronunciation over regional accidents, his posh southern vocal plays more easily than Phillips's Liverpool accent. And there may be other factors at work, such as the choices each has made about their own career, the opportunities that agents have put forward for them, and so on.

What about talent as a key factor in sustained fame for reality stars? The idea of fame as an economy often hinges on the idea that talent plays a role in assigning value to celebrity, as discussed earlier in this chapter. We might, therefore, expect that it is the most talented reality show contestants who will win their shows (in examples of competitive reality) and be go on to successful long-term careers in their field.

However, if we think about performers who have launched successful careers on the back of singing shows, for example, it is not always easy to explain why some make it and others do not – depending on what we mean by making it, of course. Some of the biggest singing stars include One Direction, Carrie Underwood, Jennifer Hudson, Little Mix and Adam Lambert. Whilst some of these high-profile acts have won reality shows, others have just been finalists or have not even made it that far.

Does their success prove that the viewing public and/or judges were wrong in anointing a particular winner and that true talent shone out? That has certainly been argued in the case of some contestants. *Project Runway* runner-up, Mondo Guerra, was seen as a fan favourite who had, according to fans and some of the show judges, more talent and potential than series winner, Gretchen Jones. That Guerra went on to win the subsequent 'all-stars' season and establish a design career on the back of the show (albeit less successfully than some alumni) was seen as a vindication of the audience perspective on what true talent looks like.

But when we consider One Direction or Susan Boyle, does this argument about talent overcoming their runner-up statuses hold weight? Whilst Boyle is clearly a talented singer, is she, objectively, a better singer than other reality stars who have had less commercial success? Even the most ardent One Direction fan would probably argue that they are not the strongest singers there have ever been (none of them even got through their *X Factor* auditions as solo artists), yet they became a global phenomenon.

We have already discussed Boyle's rise to fame through the virality of her audition, and how it was not only that audition itself, but the packaging of the audition as something that subverted the show's tropes that really cemented its importance and thus cemented Boyle in people's memories.

The marketing budget and attention that Simon Cowell and his team at Syco have put into Boyle and One Direction surely also played a key role in their success.

Then, there are reality shows that make credible stars out of several of their contestants. For example, the BBC broadcast several reality shows in conjunction with composer and musical producer, Andrew Lloyd Webber, to find new West End stars for his musicals. Most of the contestants in the final rounds of these shows have gone on to successful careers in musical theatre or television or film, regardless of where they finished – including Jessie Buckley (*Beast, Wild Rose, Chernobyl*); Samantha Barks (*Les Miserables*) and Lee Mead (*Casualty/ Holby City*). I should point out here, though, that auditionees did, often, have some level of prior training and experience – some had been minor stars in musical theatre already, others graduates of performing arts institutions like the Brit School or Sylvia Young, and therefore already came with training and contacts that may have benefitted them (although a few successful contestants did not have these advantages).

Whilst it is true that we can see examples of people who go from 'reality star' to 'celebrity', most of the time these are not two distinct statuses, but often exist alongside each other. The rise of celebrity reality formats, for example, demonstrates that reality TV is not only the preserve of ordinary people, or a quick route to fame for unknowns, but can also be a useful vehicle for a whole range of celebrities, including those whose fame is 'achieved'.

THE FAME CYCLE

So, how can we unpack this complex relationship between celebrity and reality television some more? I think it can also be useful to think about celebrity status as a *process*. By this,

Fig. 5.   The Fame Cycle.

Source: Deller, 2016.

I mean that there are stages to being famous – there is not one simple state of being a celebrity, rather a series of statuses and roles that celebrities occupy that both determine, and are determined by, the area of their fame and the practices of celebrity that they engage in. I find it helpful to visualise this process as a cycle with several stages of celebrity (Deller, 2016) from before someone achieves fame, to after that fame has waned (Fig. 5).

Different reality formats, and roles within these formats, appeal to people at different stages of this cycle. The majority of reality programming is focussed on the first of these, the 'pre-celebrity' or 'ordinary' person – both through formats that more explicitly position fame as part of the reward for participation (e.g. talent shows), or formats that claim to focus more on the everyday (e.g. docusoaps).

The second stage of fame, the *proto-celebrity*, refers to

> *a range of people in these early stages of fame,*
> *including: a celebrity's family members or partners;*

> those famous in niche or specialised fields (such as
> minority sports or glamour modelling); celetoids
> (Rojek, 2001) seeking to extend their brief moment
> of fame – such as people who have recently been
> featured on 'ordinary' reality shows and who are
> looking to cement their celebrity status; and those
> famous in one country seeking to gain recognition
> in another. (Deller, 2016, p. 376)

Proto-celebrities can commonly be found in celebrity reality formats, especially stars who have previously participated in a 'civilian' show, and therefore have some level of fame among the reality audience. However, there are also instances where people in this category may enter civilian reality shows, usually because their level of fame is deemed insufficient for a celebrity edition – or to act as a 'hook' inducing viewers to watch someone they have vaguely heard of.

The UK version of *Love Island* is a good example of this, having cast Dani Dyer, daughter of popular actor, Danny, in 2018; and in 2019, Tommy Fury (brother of boxer, Tyson) and Curtis Pritchard, a professional dancer on *Dancing With the Stars Ireland* and brother of *Strictly* professional, AJ.

There are multiple reasons why proto-celebrities are a good fit for reality television. In shows where participants are paid, these stars are unlikely to command huge fees, for one thing. For those who have previously participated in reality shows, they are already adept genre performers who know how to play to the camera. Those who are cast because of association with a more famous partner or relative can act as a 'proxy' for that star, and they bring with them the promise of potentially revealing intimate secrets about that person (especially on more confessional shows like *Celebrity Big Brother* or *I'm A Celebrity…*), or having that person in the audience to support them (e.g. on performance-based shows like *Strictly Come Dancing/Dancing With the Stars*). Proto-celebrities may bring their existing audience base to the reality show with them, but for them, the show is mostly about extending their visibility and thus their fan base – building their brand to become a more well-known celebrity with, potentially, more career opportunities following the show.

Even though we might imagine a civilian show has less status than its celebrity counterpart in terms of fame, this is not always the case. Certainly, civilian shows with high viewing figures will bring them to greater public attention than celebrity shows with low viewing figures, but there is also the question of authenticity. As we have seen already, the idea of authenticity and ordinariness a key part of the appeal of reality television and its personalities. To appear in a civilian reality show rather than a celebrity version may have the effect of making someone seem more authentic or normal, somebody who is not afraid to get their hands dirty, metaphorically (or sometimes literally depending on the show!), as an 'ordinary' person.

Proto-celebrities can also be part of the reality show genre in roles other than participants. For example, many shows use experts in a specialist field (e.g. dancing, cookery, fashion) to be advisors and mentors to participants, and this has been a route to wider fame for many of those who have taken on such roles, some of whom have enriched their professional profile in their existing area of success, others of whom have branched out into other fields, most notably television presenting (e.g. celebrity chefs, Tom Kerridge and Marcus Wareing, who took on high-profile TV judging and presenting roles following appearances in *Great British Menu*), or further reality stardom (e.g. former *Strictly Come Dancing* professionals, James Jordan and Kristina Rhianoff).

The *promotional celebrity* stage refers to participants who are taking part on reality shows essentially as a promotional

vehicle, not only for themselves (arguably all reality participants are engaged in self-promotion) but also for a company,
programme, project or organisation they are part of. Frances
Bonner notes that this is especially the case where participants
are primarily famous for appearing in another television
show on the same network, or made by the same production
company, as the reality show. Bonner (2013) notes that

> [R]eality-talent shows enable in-house promotions
> to be seen at a time when much viewing is done
> in modes which encourage the excision of ads and
> promotion slots. In this they parallel the increase
> in product placement ... the products 'placed'
> within the programmes are the other sites of the
> contestants' celebrity (p. 170)

Not all promotional celebrities are 'in-house' products.
They may also be promoting something where there might
be mutual benefits to each party of having a crossover audience. For example, stars of UK soap *Hollyoaks* have often
taken part in *Strictly Come Dancing* despite the shows being
on rival networks (Channel 4 and BBC One). The exposure
through the popular BBC One show alerts the audience to
Hollyoaks, with the hope that viewers who support a popular
contestant may then follow then on that show, whilst for the
BBC show, there is the potential of the younger *Hollyoaks*
viewer who may be enticed to watch their favourite actors
dance (Deller, 2016). Similarly, pop stars, journalists, stand-
up comedians and other non-TV celebrities may take part in
these shows to promote their 'day job'.

Whilst these celebrities can be found in all reality television formats, they are most prominent in skill-based shows,
such as *Celebrity MasterChef* or *Dancing With the Stars*
where participation occurs alongside their other endeavours (unlike residential formats such as *Big Brother* which

require several weeks away from their regular routine). In skill formats,

> *a key facet of the promotional celebrity is that they*
> *are shown in their 'day job'. This not only acts as a*
> *promotional vehicle for the star's other projects, but*
> *reminds viewers that the skill-based reality show*
> *is only interested in hard-working people. (Deller,*
> *2016, p. 379)*

Bonner (2013) notes that this may be one of the reasons why skill-based reality shows are often seen as more prestigious and attract a wider range of well-known faces than other types of reality show.

Indeed, the lower the stakes in terms of both time commitment and the chance of humiliation, the higher the calibre of promotional celebrity that can be found in reality TV. Single episode formats like charity and Christmas specials sometimes attract the kinds of celebrity usually too 'busy' to commit to a longer run. In the UK, for example, serving MPs, successful touring comedians, prominent newsreaders and television presenters with regular shows have all taken part in one-off charity specials.

Recent BBC Two series *I'll Get This* (2018) featured a group of celebrities going for a meal and taking part in various challenges (with the loser paying). It included some reality-competent performers such as Gemma Collins and Rylan Clark-Neal alongside personalities who have never taken part in more traditional reality formats, including actors, Griff Rhys Jones and Joanna Scanlon, and presenters, Victoria Coren and Josh Widdecombe. Its single-evening setting, coupled with the chance for showing off, either through excelling at the challenges or being able to easily afford the bill (which typically ranged from £500 to 1,000+) presumably made for a more attractive package to some of these stars than the months of work involved in multi-episode series.

Promotional celebrities are often supporting members of TV casts – *RuPaul's Drag Race* judges, Michelle Visage and Ross Matthews, have both taken part in versions of *Celebrity Big Brother*, for example, but it is unlikely RuPaul would be a contestant, because Ru would more comfortably fit into the next category – the *'proper'* celebrity.

This category refers to those who are at the top of their game: successful, well known and usually well regarded. These people may be household names or they may be clear experts in their field who have name recognition within that field and sometimes beyond. For these celebrities, taking part in a reality show as a contestant/participant might damage their status, implying that they are not successful enough in the day job and therefore need the extra income and exposure reality television will bring. They perhaps also have less of a strong storyline than the participants at other stages in the fame cycle-if they are already so successful, what is there to gain from taking part? As Su Holmes (2006) argues in relation to *I'm a Celebrity … Get Me Out of Here!*:

> *what apparently unites the participants, as the Executive Producer claims, is that 'they are not "really really famous" people … there's always a … question mark about why they're famous'. (p. 48)*

However, reality television still has roles for these celebrities: as presenters; judges – especially guest judges who are only required for a single week; mentors; and guest performers. High-profile names like Pharrell Williams, Katy Perry and Lady Gaga have all used reality television in this way, for example.

Taking part in an advisory role or as a guest performer allows the star to promote their most recent projects, whilst appearing as a generous benefactor bestowing their wisdom upon others. This works especially well for pop stars who are able to perform their latest single on these shows, especially in a world where TV offers little exposure for music promotion with MTV moving away from playing music videos, and the demise of music TV shows like *Top of The Pops*.

Pop stars are most usefully deployed in talent shows where their endorsement is a form of anointing the next 'big thing' (even if, once the show ends, those winners fail). In the UK version of the *X Factor*, for many years, the finalists duetted with celebrities. There was usually a significant discrepancy in the level of fame (and, arguably, talent) of the different guest performers that hinted at the preferred contestants, such as Beyoncé being paired with the eventual winner versus Westlife and Boyzone with the runners-up, and another eventual winner being paired with Kylie Minogue versus the runners-up receiving Katherine Jenkins and, hilariously, Kylie's former boyfriend and duet partner (and fellow *Neighbours* alum), Jason Donovan.

As discussed in Chapter 4, several former reality show participants have also taken these roles, including Christian Siriano (*Project Runway*), Louis Tomlinson (*X Factor*) and Jennifer Hudson (*American Idol/The Voice UK*), these returnees acting as 'proof' of reality shows as a way of discovering genuine talent – even if they are by far the exception rather than the rule.

There is one big exception to the rule that 'proper' celebrities are unlikely to take part in reality formats. Geneaology show *Who Do You Think You Are? (WDYTYA)* has attracted perhaps the starriest cast of all. For example, the UK version has attracted the likes of JK Rowling, Patrick Stewart, David Tennant and Julie Walters, whilst the US version has featured Regina King, Liv Tyler, Smokey Robinson and John Stamos. *WDYTYA's* more serious approach as a piece of historical investigation, and its emphasis on genealogical research into personal history presumably helps it attract a starry cast. In addition, each celebrity participant acts as the sole star and presenter of their episode (alongside a narrated voiceover), therefore being afforded higher 'status' than they would have within the narrative of a more traditional reality show featuring hosts, judges and multiple participants.

Even the most seemingly unlikely big names can be found in reality television. Members of the Royal family have been shown hosting charity events in connection with a reality show, for example, the Queen and *Great British Menu*, Camilla, Duchess of Cornwall, and *Strictly Come Dancing* – although for those of us who remember the ill-conceived *It's a Royal Knockout* (aka *The Grand Knockout Tournament*) the involvement of royalty is perhaps less surprising. Even Pope Francis made an appearance on reality TV when he gave a private audience to the celebrities and crew of *Pilgrimage*.

The next stage of the fame cycle, the *(re)purposed celebrity*, uses reality television as a way of adjusting their star image. They may be stars looking for a change of career, for example, athletes newly retired from the sport or actors who have recently left a high-profile TV series, or they may be celebrities who feel their public image needs some work. Celebrities who have been involved in scandal, for example, might try to use reality television as a rehabilitative process, atoning for their past sins through showing a new side to their personality (Redmond, 2011).

For example, Japanese show *Spiritual House* features celebrities having a therapeutic session with spirit guide, Hiroyuki Ehara. One episode stars retired athlete, Kazuhiro Kiyohara, who is trying to rebuild his life – and image – after being arrested on drugs charges. Through captions and narration, the show tells us he is taking part as

> *repentance for the mistake he has made... How should he face his sons, whom he has betrayed?*

> *What can he do to pay for his crime?... How can
> he pay for his sins?*

Drawing on ideas from Michel Foucault (1976), Jane Shattuc (1987) has argued that the reality TV confessional is very similar to the religious or medical version – it is a rite people need to perform in order to have their sins heard by an 'interlocutor' and thus forgiven. In Spiritual House, Kiyohara has to perform an act of confession to Ehara and, by extension, us, in order to be rehabilitated. Not only does he confess to his wrongdoings but also reveals his torment: 'It's agonising to be alive right now. It's really agonising. I really want to die, and I still do. I think about that many times in a day' (S1 E1).

By revealing the 'true' self through reality TV, it is hoped we will believe him and repurpose his star image from disgraced criminal to repentant and reformed character.

Rock star, Ozzy Osbourne, and manager wife, Sharon, were early pioneers in using reality television to repurpose the sites of their stardom. After a popular appearance on MTV's *Cribs* (which visited celebrity homes), Sharon Osbourne pitched a full reality show to MTV, where the family would be filmed round the clock at home. The result was *The Osbournes*, a reality show in the docusoap mould that had a comedic edge that made it feel like a hybrid of sitcom and reality, with much of the comedy coming from the apparent discrepancy of 'Prince of Darkness' Ozzy being a slightly bumbling father figure among a madcap home full of teenagers and pets.

Whilst *The Osbornes* ushered in a new wave of programmes focussed on the private lives of celebrities in their domestic and work environments, it was far from the first programme to do this. Morreale (2003) and Gillan (2004) trace this genre back to this the 1950s and the 'star sitcom', such as *The Adventures of Ozzie and Harriet* or *I Love Lucy*, where celebrity couples played 'themselves in fictionalised versions of their actual lives, often in replicas of their actual houses' (Gillan, 2004, p. 55).

Despite many commentators noting the comedic and heightened elements of the show as a form of fiction, the family themselves, especially Sharon, were keen to emphasise its claims to reality:

> *You got used to the crew being there. It was a bit like being at school, there are all these other people around, but you're not really aware of them. You just get on with your work… There were no scripts. Never. Not one. How could anyone ever script Ozzy? (Osbourne, 2005, pp. 293, 313)*

This desire to emphasise the 'realness' of the show may well be connected to Sharon Osbourne's enduring brand. Coming out of *The Osbournes*, she was able to reinvent her star image by taking on a series of television commitments, most visibly reality show judging. She describes how her first major judging role, on The *X Factor* (UK) helped transform her image beyond her marriage and *The Osbournes*: 'I was no longer thought of primarily as Ozzy's wife, I was now "Sharon Osbourne, *X Factor* judge" ' (Osbourne, 2005, p. 346). By maintaining the impression of the 'real' nature of *The Osbournes*, she is able to translate that to her other reality shows, presenting herself as an honest, authentic, and therefore credible, judge. (Daughter Kelly has been able to do the same with her own reality presenting and judging roles in shows like *Project Catwalk* and *Project Runway Junior*).

Whilst Osbourne's example is an extreme way of using reality television to repurpose one's career, it has been a useful strategy for many celebrities. Success in cookery shows like *Celebrity MasterChef* has led several former contestants (including comedian, Hardeep Singh Koli, and actress, Lisa

Faulkner) to rebrand themselves as food experts, for example. Winners of *Strictly Come Dancing* and *Dancing with the Stars* have gone on to roles as judges on these and other reality shows. Former Catatonia singer, Cerys Matthews, took advantage of her renewed visibility after an appearance on *I'm a Celebrity...* and has rebranded herself as a music expert and broadcaster, with popular shows on BBC Radios 2 and 6Music (Deller, 2016) – and there are many more examples like these.

Sometimes, the motivations for repurposing star image are not made explicit by the celebrities themselves during these shows, or the pre-publicity, but inferred by journalists and viewers who follow the career trajectories of the famous. However, the searching for a renewed purpose to their stardom can sometimes explicitly form part of the narrative for these stars. In BBC 2 show *Pilgrimage*, a social experiment programme seeing celebrities walk religious pilgrimage routes, athlete, Greg Rutherford, spoke directly to camera about his recent retirement from professional sports and the crisis of identity this had plunged him into. Whilst having his hair cut by Marcello, a retired barber who was hosting the group at his retreat centre, Rutherford confessed:

> *for me, my passion was always sports, and I was lucky enough to become a professional track and field athlete. Now I'm 31 and I'm retired and I'm essentially in a situation where I need to find a new job.*

Interlocutor Marcello tells him he has been a champion and does not need to worry. Through tears, Rutherford reveals to camera the emotional impact of this confessional moment:

> *The fact that he told me I have been a champion and I will find something else to succeed at is*

something I appreciate hearing. I don't know
what the next path is, I'm trying to find what the
next path is, and I guess as a sportsperson when
you're trying to redefine yourself, you realise your
best days are gone, so having something else to fill
that void is one of the biggest things I'm gonna
experience.

Funnily enough, Rutherford's involvement in several reality shows since retiring hints that his ideal repurposing may well be as a television personality.

Finally, there is the *post celebrity*. These are celebrities who are no longer actively visible and successful in their previous line of work. Some of them may still be working in this field in a diminished capacity (e.g. pop stars on the 'reunion circuit'), but they are no longer at the height of their fame. These kinds of stars are those who might feature in 'whatever happened to' articles, or who may be referred to as 'has-beens'. They do, however, still have a level of public recognition, and their presence in reality shows is often a way of audiences speculating on life after fame. For some, this may also provide a career boost, either restoring them to their previous arena of fame or helping them to re-purpose themselves.

It is possible for people to go from post celebrity to pre-celebrity, that is, to have become so un-famous that they need to re-enter 'civilian' reality shows, and there are several examples where this has been the case, although very often their previous brushes with fame are brought up by the TV producers. Occasionally, this has led to a career boost, but more often than not, they are rejected, 'sealing the lid on participants' fame narratives and condemning them back to permanent obscurity' (Deller, 2016, p. 383).

Although this 'fame cycle' is often a linear process, sometimes celebrities might skip certain stage altogether; they might remain in one stage; they might move back and forth between stages or even occupy a couple of stages simultaneously.

You will also notice that there is stage in the centre of the model, the *pro-reality celebrity*. This refers to celebrities who make a living as reality television stars and spend their time going from one show to another. Some celebrities spend their whole career in this state (e.g. Gemma Collins, Farrah Abraham), some move into it as a change of career (e.g. Brigitte Nielsen, Janice Dickinson), some go back and forth between this and other stages (e.g. Goldie, Bonang Matheba), and some may be in this stage for a short whilst, but exit after a few reality appearances if they have managed to find a successful transition (back) to another area of fame (e.g. Sue Perkins, Caroline Flack).

When a celebrity reality programme works, it is not only beneficial for its stars (whether in terms of income, exposure, a life-changing experience or new career opportunities) but also offers plenty of enjoyment for audiences:

> *it offers viewers a range of interesting narratives: conflict between participants; discussions about the nature of fame (both its attractions and its problems); and the conflicting dynamics of the 'ordinary' and the 'special', of the talented and the talentless. (Deller, 2016, p. 385)*

> *On [the] one hand, such programming aims to uncover extra levels of extraordinary talent among existing television personalities, often as a cross-promotional device for the same network, all the while reinforcing audience empathy with the stars' ordinary human struggles to overcome new challenges. On the other hand, audiences are given additional opportunities for what Jeffrey Sconce*

(2004, p. 453) calls 'celebrity schadenfreude',
in which we get to spectate as minor stars of
questionable talent make fools of themselves,
disproving any claim to extraordinary status.
(Payne, 2009, p. 297)

CONCLUSION

There are no guarantees in the world of reality TV celebrity. It can transport 'ordinary people' to a world of fame and fortune, but it can also give them a level of public visibility they do not actually want. It can give celebrities a new lease of life, but it can also ruin their reputation. It can be educative, but it can also be very silly (it would be hard to argue that seeing celebrities eating kangaroo anus on *I'm a Celebrity* or being chased by a pack of dogs in *Release the Hounds* has any point beyond humiliation and the stars demonstrating that they are 'good sports'!).

However, as Barron (2015) notes, what reality TV is really about is blurring the lives between public and private, our front- and back-stage selves. A former *Big Brother* and *I'm a Celebrity* producer once claimed that 'With normal Big Brother we're making ordinary people extraordinary. With this, we're making famous people very, very ordinary' (Phil Edgar Jones cited in Biressi & Nunn, 2005, p. 147). I would argue that it is more about highlighting that the boundaries between ordinary and extraordinary are always in flux – and the interplay between the two is what gives reality TV, whether celebrity or 'civilian', its core appeal.

In Chapter 6, we will see how some of these ideas have been extended further into a format that complicates the private and public divide as much as reality TV – social media.

6

REALITY TELEVISION IN AN AGE OF SOCIAL MEDIA

As I started writing this book, in autumn 2018, my reality television viewing experience was dominated by the arrival of one new reality show and the departure of another. On September 14, a new set of housemates entered the UK *Big Brother* house, and broadcaster Channel 5 announced that they would be the final ever housemates of the UK edition. Four days later, on *BB*'s former home of Channel 4, another set of 'ordinary' people moved into a property in the initial series of *The Circle*.

When *Big Brother* launched, a key component of the marketing in many countries was the idea that viewers could follow action 24/7 via a series of live feed cameras on the show's website. It is easy to forget that this was a bold move at the time, with broadband yet to be installed in most people's homes. I distinctly remember logging in periodically to the *Big Brother* website to watch live streaming of that initial series through a very buffery dial-up connection! The aim of the live camera feeds was to enhance the experience of everything participants did being available for scrutiny, the cameras acting as 'proof' of the reality of the format.

Watching live camera feeds pre-empted the 'always-on' cultures of social media for several viewers. Mark Andrejevic (2004) notes that early viewers would watch at work,

> *alternating between job tasks, watching the*
> *live internet feeds from the* Big Brother *house,*
> *and sending intermittent messages to one of*
> *the online chat rooms ... all three activities*
> *could take place on the same computer monitor.*
> *Consequently, the online video feeds came to*
> *serve, in some cases, as the visual equivalent of*
> *background music, providing kinetic 'wallpaper'*
> *for the desktops of people keeping track of the*
> *action in the* Big Brother *house while they were*
> *working (p. 63)*

However, the *BB* live feed has a complex history. Most obviously, the central idea that the camera feeds captured everything as it happened proved to not be the case in most territories. There were only cameras in some parts of the house shown, and there was often a slight delay between live action in the house and what was shown on the feed, allowing for producers to block out certain content – usually, things like celebrity gossip, talking about brands other than a show's commercial partners or housemates singing popular songs. Regular *Big Brother* fans quickly became used to the sound of birdsong over images of housemates chatting!

The accessibility of live feeds also varied – some countries never really embraced the live feed element, others removed it entirely, much to the chagrin of viewers. One of the producers of *BB* Australia, Alex Mavroidakis, explained their reasons for taking down the live feed as part of a fan site Q&A, including the assertion that the internet feed might damage the television property:

> *Despite popular opinion, live streaming the* Big
> Brother *House is no viable – economically and*
> *ethically. A lot has changed and not just in Australia.*
> *Reduced feeds of the House has been a shift*
> *globally. We want you to tune in to* Big Brother *the*
> *TV show, not a fixed camera quad split of a house*
> *with people lounging about … Behind* Big Brother
> *members must remember – you are the hardcore*
> *– the purists – I am like you. I want BB on 24/7*
> *all the time everywhere I go. But the fact is that*
> *in 8 years we streamed live in Australia practically*
> *nobody watched it! (Behind* Big Brother, *2013)*

Several territories that retained live feeds took the approach of monetising them – charging fans to watch this extra material. For example, in the USA, access to the live feeds (at the time of writing) is rolled into the paid-for CBS 'All Access' pass (which includes streaming of CBS shows). The promotional material reads:

- Stream the Live Feeds 24/7* starting on June 26, 9/8c.

- Watch the Houseguests from every angle.

- Chat with other fans + enjoy subscriber exclusives.

- Watch full episodes on demand.

  (*May be edited, delayed, or blacked out on occasion, CBS, 2019).

Access to this paratextual content is now denied to the ordinary television viewer, whereas subscribers can get the 'full story', including the opportunity to engage with other fans on the official online platform (a curiously quaint idea given the accessibility of social media and unofficial forum sites where fans can easily find one another without spending money!).

Big Brother's use of the internet to provide connection between audiences and the show means its viewers have a completely opposite *BB* experience to the housemates, who are cut off from all entertainment and connection with the outside world. Whilst the internet was marketed as a key part of the viewing experience, it was entirely absent from the experience of the participants, as if it did not even exist. (Although this premise was somewhat undermined in some later series of *BB* where viewer comments on social media were sometimes used to give housemates clues about their reception).

The example of *Big Brother* and its live feeds illustrates some of the key tensions in the relationship between reality TV and the internet – are they allies or competitors? Which provides the 'truest' story'? And, how does each influence the other?

REALITY TV IN THE INTERNET ERA

The histories of reality television and the internet are largely intertwined. Whilst both have their foundations in the mid-twentieth century, they became household fixtures around the turn of the millennium and have become an inescapable part of culture ever since.

The revelatory techniques of reality television, its surveillance culture and democratisation of fame have all arguably paved the way for the self-presentation modes employed online. Vlogs, blogs, social media 'stories', status updates and 'snaps' all provide ways for us to document both the mundane and the extraordinary alongside each other, as often as we wish to. In addition, the apparent 'democracy' of many social media platforms where megastars have a presence alongside 'ordinary' people, and where those 'ordinary' people can become megastars themselves, follows where reality TV led in blurring the boundaries between celebrity and civilian (Abidin, 2018; Marwick & Boyd, 2011; Senft, 2013).

Yet, there are also claims that the internet, especially the rise of video-based platforms, such as YouTube, TikTok and InstagramTV, has impacted the viewership of television, especially among young people (Oakes, 2019). So, how are reality shows coping with this challenge for attention?

FROM TELEVISION VIEWING TO MULTIMEDIA EXPERIENCES

The formal boundaries between 'television' and the 'internet' are increasingly blurred. TV sets can show YouTube and social media content, streaming and catch-up services are reliant on internet connections and TV apps are available on mobile phones. Broadcasters and production companies no longer just make television programmes, they make multimedia brands – it is rare to encounter a TV show that does not engage with social media – and reality shows are some of the most visibly active in extending their storylines, content and marketing across multiple platforms.

Whilst it is difficult to find the point at which 'television' ends and the 'internet' begins, for the sake of convenience, I'm including long-form video streaming content on platforms like Netflix and Amazon Prime in the category of 'television' and content native to YouTube and other video sharing platforms (as opposed to traditional TV shows that have been uploaded to said platforms) as 'internet' or social media.

Reality television does not simply exist in the form of broadcast episodes. Whilst the TV episodes are still privileged as the primary site of 'action', the action is extended through a range of paratexts– extra media that complement the main programmes. Social media paratexts are a core part of the marketing strategy for most reality shows, and official social media content can be found on a range of social media platforms. To get the full experience of, say, *Love Island* or *RuPaul's Drag Race*, means not only watching the show and its spin-offs, buying merchandise or reading interviews with the stars, but also connecting with the shows on YouTube, Facebook, Twitter, Instagram, SnapChat, their official apps and more.

For example, the Kardshian/Jenner family have become experts at extending their presence into a range of paratexts. To fully follow the stories associated with them, it is not sufficient simply to watch the reality show *Keeping Up With the Kardashians* – there are spin-off TV shows, apps, interviews in newspapers and magazines, and innumerable social media accounts for each member of the family – including accounts for all their various business endeavours – for example, their fashion and beauty brands. They carefully coordinate their marketing strategy so that content is not purely repetitive across the different platforms, but each induces you to engage with the next. Typically, they will share a small clip of video out of context with a reminder to watch the next episode of their show, or a still from a photo shoot to induce readers to purchase a magazine.

To further complicate matters, not only do TV shows themselves have official accounts on social media but content about them is also created and circulated by the production companies making them, the broadcasters showing them, their presenters, participants (past and present) and members of the production team. These shows are not single 'texts' but rather sprawling multimedia entities, even before we get on to the way audiences also play a role in creating, circulating and remixing content online!

DEVISING SOCIAL MEDIA STRATEGIES

In Chapter 4, I discussed the example of Susan Boyle on *Britain's Got Talent* and explored how her success was largely due to the fact that she was an example of the show subverting its own tropes. That alone would have no doubt made her a star in the UK. But she would never have become a global sensation without the internet. Whilst it was the content and format that resonated globally, it was the speed and reach of the YouTube clip that turned her into a phenomenon.

Boyle was an early example of a viral sensation, where something is shared and re-shared until it has an enormous reach. The 'spreadability' of content (Jenkins, Ford, & Green, 2013) has long been part of the success of reality television – think back to the confrontation between 'Nasty Nick' and Craig in the first series of *Big Brother* UK, for example – with reality moments, characters and storylines bleeding into newspapers, magazines, radio and other television shows (see Chapter 2), but the internet capitalises on this potential.

Boyle's success demonstrates the power of social media to expand the reach of reality television – a viral clip like this does not only attempt to draw viewers to the source show *Britain's Got Talent*, but highlights *Got Talent* as a franchise – the next Susan Boyle could be in your country's edition. It turned Boyle into a marketable commodity, her music having the potential to make many more millions from global fame than it would from national fame. And there is also the lucrative advertising revenue earned from the YouTube clip!

But what goes into creating social media content for reality shows in the first place? Paul Kelly is the Social Media Coordinator for Core Content, an Irish production company responsible for a portfolio of factual and reality shows including *First Dates Ireland, The Unemployables* and *Don't Tell the Bride Ireland*. He describes his role as 'to utilise new media, social media and digital technologies to support the primary programmes and provide audiences with a richer and more engaging entertainment experience' (personal interview). This role involves a range of activities – not only devising and implementing social media strategies for marketing but also providing extra content not shown on television and managing the online casting process.

One of the core strategies for Core's social media is to target the 18–35 audience who are less likely to watch TV as it is broadcast:

> *A lot of our strategies focus on the fragmentation and distribution of content for these audiences – this includes pulling specific highlight clips from the primary programme and repacking them as shorter, more shareable content pieces for social media …. We're aware that not as many young people sit down in front of their television at the scheduled time of broadcast, and we're facilitating them by making the content available in short online clips, and by driving audiences to the VOD [video on-demand] platforms where they can watch the full programmes in their own time.*

However, social media content is not solely there to drive viewers to the VOD platforms, but to keep existing viewers engaged and offer them something extra:

> *We try to listen to genuine viewer feedback as an indicator of what information they value or desire yet may be missing from the primary programme. Using* First Dates *as an example, viewers often tweet to ask what happened with participants/daters after their televised dates. With this in mind, we developed the 'Dater Update'*

> *video update series to go out after each episode*
> *in which we share up-to-date video updates from*
> *the daters themselves .... These sort of comments*
> *are very valuable to us as they let us know what*
> *extratextual information to provide fans in order*
> *to enrich their viewing experience... the aim [of*
> *social media strategies is] to use digital media*
> *to supplement the primary text with the sort of*
> *extratextual material that provides information,*
> *boosts to the story and/or adds value to the*
> *audience's experience.*

The social media strategy described here by Paul Kelly is a natural extension of other forms of reality TV paratexts like spin-off shows and tie-in books, which places viewer engagement with these shows beyond the confines of broadcasting schedules or sought-out media. Social media content can appear alongside updates from friends, family, news agencies and other brands in users' feeds, keeping them constantly updated without the need to explicitly seek out information by watching a spin-off or seeking out a brand's website.

There can also be opportunities to extend partnerships with commercial sponsors into the online realm. In the case of Core's makeover show *Home Rescue*:

> *In partnership with the programme sponsors,*
> *IKEA, we shot a series of 3 to 5-minute long,*
> *interactive 360° video tours of each of the homes*
> *for Facebook. These videos gave viewers a 360°*
> *view of the rooms, which they could interact with*
> *and inspect by moving their phones around while*
> *the show's presenter and interior designer guided*
> *them through the rooms, explaining the story of the*
> *designs in more detail.*

Successful social media paratexts extend the feeling of a programme (Booth, 2010; Deller, 2014b; Gray, 2010), whether that is through providing informative material, such as the house tours described above, or extending the playfulness of the TV narrative by sharing memes, jokes and referencing fan theories – as we will see later in this chapter.

When it comes to devising a social media strategy for a TV show, there can be a complex collaboration between production companies and broadcasters. In the case of Core Content, this involves Paul Kelly devising the overall strategy and then liaising with key stakeholders:

> *Ongoing and close collaboration with the*
> *production team is important in terms of*
> *maintaining a tone, aesthetic, editorial direction,*
> *etc…, we achieve this consistency by maintaining*
> *a relatively robust approval process in which all*
> *digital content connected to the programme is*
> *approved by a member of the production team*
> *before being shared anywhere publicly… Generally*
> *the strategy is heavily coordinated with the channel*
> *showing our programmes.*

The level of co-ordination and synchronisation across different related social media accounts for the same programme varies wildly. Core's strategy is about maintaining a consistent approach to content and branding, something emulated by World of Wonder, makers of *RuPaul's Drag Race*, who share similar (and sometimes identical) content on social media whether through the WOW account, those of the individual shows, or the broadcasters. For example, the same promotional shots and branding for *RuPaul's Drag Race UK* appeared across social media accounts for WOW, broadcaster BBC Three and the official show account. In contrast, completely different formats and content are used to promote *Queer Eye* on the social media accounts for the show itself, Netflix and its production company (ITV Studios).

The tone of reality shows, the audience they attract and the way they are perceived by other media varies – and the same is true of their social media. For example, *Love Island*'s social media feeds include plenty of jokes amongst information and soliciting viewer opinions, whilst *American Idol*'s are more about promotion and information:

- Every time Ovie doesn't say 'MESSAGE!' a butterfly dies. #LoveIsland.

- Maura would like to thank her underwear guardian angel at this moment in time. #LoveIsland.

- Auditions for #TheNextIdol start NOW! Come see us TODAY at the Brooklyn Expo Center! Contestant registration begins at 7am. Walk-ups are welcome!

- Don't miss #AmericanIdol mentor @mrBobbyBones compete on #CelebrityFamilyFeud this Sunday on @ABCNetwork at 8|7c!

Not all social media platforms are the same, and they offer different benefits for audiences and broadcasters. In the case of Core Content:

> *Each platform has its own benefits and drawbacks .... It usually depends on the content, the message and the limitations of the platform. For example, a two-minute episode highlight clip couldn't be shared to Instagram (although it could be shared on IGTV) because Instagram limits video length to no longer than 60-seconds. Similarly, posting in real-time when a show is on air wouldn't work as well on Facebook as it does on Twitter...*

Facebook tends to be our best performer in terms of shareability. It consistently generates the best reach for our content. If we want a clip to spread, Facebook is our preferred channel. If we have news that we want to share or an announcement to make, again Facebook provides a platform for us to reach the widest audience. It's also particularly good for casting callouts. People will share, comment, react, tag friends and generally engage quite heavily on Facebook…

Instagram tends to work for shorter, snackable, eye-catching and humorous content, as well as behind-the-scenes style content. Again, while it's dependent on the programme itself, memes, short snippets and images that lean more towards the light-hearted side, tend to perform well on Instagram. Behind-the-scenes style content – sneak peaks, shots from on set, ongoings from the COCO offices, etc. – tends to work quite well here as well, particularly through the Instagram stories feature. Fans of the shows tend to engage well with that content.

YouTube is more about evergreen content. Clips tend to work particularly well on YouTube. Generally, standout moments from episodes are shared on YouTube as highlights. YouTube's search functions and recommendation systems benefit the sharing of clips that will not only spread initially, but that viewers will continue to find and return to over time. (Paul Kelly, personal interview)

TECHNOLOGIES FOR TALKING TELLY

As we have seen in Chapter 2, reality television is a genre that is designed to elicit talk and shared opinions. Its claims of holding up a mirror to human behaviour and interaction naturally extend to audiences critiquing the actions they see on screen, not only in terms of judging the participants' behaviours but also by speculating on the authenticity of what they are watching. This talk is not only found in homes, workplaces and schools, but also proliferates online in forums, web comments, blogs, vlogs and social media. With the emergence of 'Web 2.0' technologies and the rise in participatory culture (Jenkins, 2006), reality show chat filled up blogs, forums and message boards.

Brands like (the now-deceased) *Television Without Pity (TWOP)* and *Digital Spy* cut their teeth on reality television, becoming go-to hangouts where viewers could discuss favourite shows. Such talk involves a wide range of activity, including: identifying heroes and villains amongst the cast; predicting storylines, events and outcomes; creating fantasy leagues of past contestants; imagining ideal casts, tasks or presenters; writing fan fiction; sharing community in-jokes; discussing conspiracy theories; creating voting campaigns; and heavily critiquing every aspect of a show's production and editing (Andrejevic, 2008; Gray, 2005).

Alongside forums, recaps and liveblogs of episodes became a staple feature of online culture, with mainstream sites such as *The Guardian* and *Vulture* joining fan blogs and audience-oriented sites like *TWOP* in sharing humorous takes on shows, either as broadcast in the case of a liveblog, or shortly after with recap blogs. As we saw in Chapter 2, engaging in 'snark', hate-watching and critique demonstrates both an investment in the television show, and the desire to engage with, and entertain, readers. In his study of *TWOP*, Mark Andrejevic (2008) notes that, in some cases, people follow shows through recaps alone, rather than viewing them, 'because the recaps were entertaining and thorough enough to stand on their own' (p. 32)

It is here that I should hold my hand up to my own role in this culture – for several years, I wrote TV reviews and previews for *Lowculture*, a now-defunct entertainment site with a rich vein of humour with a strong reality show component, and I was also part of a team running several snarky recap blogs where we would affectionately (mostly!) mock the tropes of the reality shows we were watching. Whilst this was at first a fun way to entertain ourselves and our readers, making fun of the shows we watched whilst also critiquing aspects of these programmes, life (or cancellation) got in the way of recapping most of the programmes – and in the case of *The X Factor UK*, we gave up once we realised the show was even more cynical than we were, and that there was no longer any pleasure or entertainment in sitting through its increasingly long shows to make the same jokes about a programme that had become 'a rehash of a rehash of itself'.

By the mid-late 2000s, forums and blogs had competitors for audience attention in the form of social media sites. MySpace, Facebook and especially Twitter had become environments where people not only interacted with friends and family but also shared content relating to their interests. They quickly became a place for online communities to form, whether in structurally organised ways like Facebook groups, or through more loose aggregations such as people following a hashtag on Twitter. Whilst social media has not meant the death of forums and blogs, there are certainly fewer than before: for example, *Television Without Pity* ceased operation in 2017, and The *Guardian*'s commitment to live blogging and recapping reality shows has scaled down in recent years: they still support *The Great British Bake Off* and *Strictly Come Dancing*, but have stopped covering several other reality shows, including The *X Factor* and *The Apprentice*.

There are several potential reasons why social media has proved an attractive space for talk about reality (and other) television, though perhaps the biggest are its ubiquity, and its centralisation of content. It is much easier to concentrate discussion of social, professional and personal interests across a few social media platforms than multiple forums and blogs.

TWEETING WITH THE TELLY

Whilst all social media platforms contain reality TV content, it is worth discussing Twitter in some more detail as the platform where interaction from TV viewers is most encouraged. This inducement to participate is less about engaging with extra 'value added' content such as behind the scenes or what happened next footage (which are of key importance to YouTube, Facebook and official websites), but more about tweeting along with the programme as you are watching, ideally at the time of broadcast.

Following a television show on Twitter whilst it is being broadcast can be an exhilarating and exhausting experience. Whilst the traffic varies dramatically from show to show, reality television tends to be one of the most popular talking points on the platform (Bruns, 2011; Deller, 2011; Woodford, 2013), and thousands of tweets can come in during the duration of a single show. There are several reasons why this is. Firstly, reality is a genre that privileges 'liveness', especially in shows that are broadcast live and implement some form of voting. 'Liveness' helps the media emphasise its role as something that can unite society:

> *liveness – that is, live transmission – guarantees a*
> *potential connection to our shared social realities*
> *as they are happening ... 'Liveness' naturalises the*
> *idea that, through the media, we achieve a shared*
> *attention to the realities that matter for us as a*
> *society. This is the idea of the media as social frame,*
> *the myth of the mediated centre. It is because of this*
> *underlying idea (suggesting society as a common*
> *space focused around a 'shared' ritual centre) that*
> *watching something 'live' makes the difference it*
> *does: otherwise why should we care that others are*
> *watching the same image as us, and (more or less)*
> *when we are? (Couldry, 2003, pp. 97–99)*

As discussed in Chapter 2, by emphasising their liveness, some reality shows present themselves as a shared social experience where different generations can congregate, either in person or facilitated by technology. When it comes to Twitter's role in this process, the liveness is hyped up by hashtags on screen throughout broadcast, and sometimes through verbal inducements from presenters to take part in discussion. This hype also extends to official social media accounts run by broadcasters, production companies, presenters and participants (including former participants) promoting live tweets during the show and often offering live Q&A immediately following broadcast:

> *Obviously Twitter comes to life when programmes*
> *are on air because it's where people go to react in*
> *real-time. I'm sure it goes without saying that live*
> *tweeting is our priority for Twitter. It's all about*
> *engaging in and monitoring online conversations*
> *when a programme is on air. (Paul Kelly)*

One of the draws of Twitter is the presence not only of other members of the audience but also official accounts and those of producers, hosts, experts and participants – and fellow celebrities who also tweet their viewing (Deller, 2011). These all contribute to the sense of watching via social media being a communal event, and one that ideally takes place as a show is broadcast. The visibility of reality shows on Twitter and other social media also means that watching and engaging online in real time is the best way for viewers to avoid spoilers. Not all Twitter discussion happens live, of course, and there is often a distinction between those who tweet live and those who do not, with live tweets often only making sense to other viewers who are watching at the same time:

> *IS THIS WHO WANTS TO BE A FUCKING MILLIONAIRE??? #LoveIsland*

> *But I thought he has nothing to stay for? Why hasn't he left #LoveIsland*

Twitter commentary on social media platforms can involve a range of content, from opinions and reactions, to simply saying they are watching a show:

> *Amber's been a brave girl. Kudos #LoveIsland*

> *Back from the best chilled week on holiday. A day in bed catching up on 9 eps of #LoveIsland*

Commercial brands can also use hashtags of popular programmes as a way of marketing their own services, sometimes circumventing the convention to post #ad or #spon to indicate an advert, by making it look as though their content is a natural part of the conversation rather than a marketing ploy, or even just using a popular hashtag in a tweet that has nothing to do with the programme in question:

> *Let our client @[Business name] recreate a #LoveIsland look for you. VIP at-home hair and makeup service.*

#LoveIsland We are an organization that provides consulting services in quality standards, strategic road safety plans and energy efficiency. Visit our website.

HUMOUR, MEMES AND GIFS

Reality television as a genre lends itself very well to humour. Many shows incorporate humour into their style and approach (see Chapter 4), and audiences have long used humour in their discussions, both offline (see Chapter 2) and online. Social media discussion of reality shows is full of puns, quips, animated gifs, memes and sarcastic commentary as audiences perform for the kudos of likes and shares. Popular reality franchises like *Drag Race* and *Love Island* even have multiple fan accounts that just share jokes and memes about the shows. For certain reality brands, humour is a key component of their social media, and they both create their own jokes and memes and re-circulate those made by fans. Indeed, some shows can almost appear desperate to be laughed at, given the frequency with which they post such content.

This can lead to an interesting tension when official accounts associated with TV shows try to capitalise on humour. As audience jokes can be quite critical towards the shows, the jokes shared by official accounts may not be reflective of the humour within the audience commentary – meaning that not only are they privileging certain (less critical) voices above others but may also misunderstand what it is about their shows that viewers find hilarious.

Perhaps, the most popular reality show memes and GIFs of all, however, are those that take on a life of their own, with key lines, scenes and expressions being adopted as memes that are re-circulated and take on new meaning far beyond their original source (Shifman, 2013) – think of the picture of Gordon Ramsay yelling at a *Hell's Kitchen* contestant that became the 'This Meal is so Unfinished' meme, or the GIF of Tyra Banks yelling at *America's Next Top Model* contestant, Tiffany Richardson, that 'we were all rooting for you' (Blackmon, 2017). Memes like these give these moments a much longer afterlife than the shows themselves even have.

Memes are only one example of the way the internet can extend the life of reality shows and their participants. As discussed in Chapter 3, the advent of streaming services and other online video platforms has opened up archives of reality television to new viewers as well as long-term fans wanting to re-watch old favourites. Add to this the hundreds of wikis, blogs and forums dedicated to reality television, and we can see that reality television is far from an ephemeral phenomenon, but can have long-term impacts on viewers, the industry and participants.

REALITY PARTICIPANTS AND SOCIAL MEDIA

Most reality participants now encounter the issue of how to approach social media – which platforms to use, how to use them and what they want to get out of using them.

There is an increased expectation that reality show participants will already have an online presence before a show begins, and (as long as there are no embargoes on revealing their participation) they often use these channels to build hype before a show starts, and throughout their journey. If a participant is away from social media (e.g. in a residential format like *Big Brother* or *The Circle*), they will often hand over accounts to friends and family to drum up support on their behalf.

The people I interviewed for this book had very different experiences of what producers wanted from them in terms of social media engagement, from programmes focussing on more personal journeys suggesting people made accounts private, to competitive shows actively encouraging them to promote the programme through those channels:

> *They had a social media expert who gave us advice, they were quite responsible. They advised us to put it on private, but you didn't have to if you didn't want to. I chose not to because I'm out there, I'm an educator and an activist and I'm quite tough mentally. The only thing I did was make my Facebook friends-only. They said it'll be 95% positive and only 5% negative – it's easy to focus on the 5%., but don't respond to it, don't feed the trolls. I went on Twitter afterwards and it seemed to add up to what they said, those percentages. There was some negative, but I didn't need to respond to it because all the allies shut them down. (Observational show participant)*

> *I hadn't done Twitter or Facebook up until then and we were encouraged to that. We weren't forced, but it was encouraged. And it was quite nice, actually, to be able to interact with people and when something happens... when stuff had gone wrong... it's lovely to see the reaction from people at that point. (*The Great British Bake Off *participant)*

> *We also offer a set of written guidelines for contributors in advance of their appearances on our programmes. We caution them about to the risk of receiving negative comments online. Our general advice to contributors is to avoid looking at any sort of online commentary when their show goes to air: Don't check Twitter when*

*their show is on air; Don't check the comment
sections of any clips or content that might involve
them; Don't Google themselves; etc. We advise
contributors to make their social media accounts
less discoverable or private. In the case that they
are exposed to negative comments, we remind them
that negative comments generally come from just
a small subsection of viewers and that they're not
necessarily true, nor do they reflect the opinion of
all viewers. We also strongly recommend that they
don't engage with them. (Paul Kelly, Core Content)*

Most participants had experienced people contacting them
on social media or via email:

*They loved me! I was definitely the people's fave. I
actually still have people DM me now – eight years
later – to ask why I haven't been on any other TV
show yet. (Claudia, Sorority Girls)*

*We've had like thousands and thousands of emails
back… from every continent across the world
because somehow it got onto YouTube …. There
were about a third who … hated it, about a third
who were 'wow it was amazing' … and about a
third who were asking questions. (Observational
participants)*

Whilst these interactions had often proved a positive experience for participants, there can be drawbacks with engaging in social media discussion for participants and producers alike:

*It's a paradise of the opinionated … once you look
it's like Pandora's box … you aren't that kind of
person, but you discover everybody in the country*

thinks you are that person. (Social experiment participant)

I wanted them to see the truth of it [their representation] and they couldn't see it and I knew it was no good me trying to explain it. (Observational participant)

It's an unfortunate side effect of the internet that reality TV participants are now potentially more easily exposed to negative comments and opinions expressed by viewers online. Viewers can be quick to forget that the comments they make online are about real people, and that those real people may well see the comments and be genuinely affected by them. It's something that we're aware of and that we look to prevent. We're not necessarily against people expressing their opinions about our programmes and contributors – it's what makes the sort of online discussions that circulate around our programmes so exciting and dynamic – but we draw a line when comments become excessively negative, hurtful, abusive or potentially overwhelming. We have a policy of monitoring conversations, and hiding/reporting any comments that cross the line, and blocking users who are abusive. (Paul Kelly)

Social media also offers participants a chance of extending their moment of fame from their celetoid moment, and it can also be an opportunity for income generation. Participants in skill-based shows like *Project Runway* and *Great British Menu* can use social media as a platform for their businesses, but there are also opportunities for people to earn income through advertising and endorsements, as evidenced in the number of reality contestants who go on to post sponsored content on their social media in the same vein as internet influencers (Abidin, 2018).

Social media also affords participants a chance to share their 'authentic' take on the shows they have taken part in. They can use the platform to promote the brand long after their own participation, and act as promotional vehicles for current and upcoming initiatives. *RuPaul's Drag Race* stars, for example, often remain brand ambassadors long after their initial TV appearances through taking part in official events like Drag Con (a spin-off convention from the show), and also through various tours and public appearances with other queens from the show, all of which are heavily promoted on social media. The official *Drag Race* accounts continue to promote the endeavours of their graduates in between seasons, as well as the queens supporting the TV show, and thus the brand extends the discourse of the programme of a drag 'family', 'proving' through their social media accounts that *Drag Race* is not only a TV show but also a community.

Social media gives participants the opportunity to tell us 'what happened next' and keep us interested in their story. Remember Tom from *Queer Eye* (Chapter 4)? The show left him hopeful of a reunion with ex-wife, Abby, and through his social media accounts, viewers followed their engagement and subsequent remarriage.

Participants also use social media to give their view of 'what really happens' on a show, especially if they perceive they were mis-edited. The huge difference between the presentation of self on social media and reality television is the power an individual has over the content. As discussed in Chapters 2–4, one of the chief complaints about reality television, from both audiences and participants, is the way in which it is edited. Contestants' social media critiques of their representation often sit alongside confessional autobiographies and tell-all interviews bemoaning the way they were presented and claiming the 'truth' lies in the footage left on the cutting room floor. Social media is no less curated and edited – but the editing comes from the individual and the way they choose to present themselves, rather than the way others have chosen to present them:

> *Surely it's going to be dead soon? When will people realise how it affects those involved and how fake it is? – Joe Conaboy,* X Factor[1]

> *You don't know me. You saw 45 minutes that's edited for the benefit of the show. That's not me – Lewis Flanagan,* Big Brother[2]

We see the notions of 'reality' and 'authenticity' again coming into play with social media acting as a means of verifying (or otherwise) the truth claims of reality shows. The idea of participants acting without the editing mechanisms of the TV production process can give an impression of the 'truth', revealing what the cameras did not. However, the reverse can also be argued, that is, participants' views are highly subjective and the camera acts as a more 'objective' witness to events without the filter of individual feeling.

REALITY TV'S INFLUENCE ON THE INTERNET

Whilst this chapter has so far focussed on social media's impact on reality television, it is worth remembering that reality television's techniques have paved the way for many of the forms of self-presentation we see online. Even back in 2004, Mark Andrejevic noted that 'we are increasingly exposed to innovative uses of digital media that allow us to make our own reality shows' (p. 61), through the spread of technologies like webcams to domestic users. This enabled the rise of webcam culture and the self-revelatory practices of 'camgirls' like Jennifer Ringley, aka Jennicam, who broadcast all aspects of her daily life online (Senft, 2008). Webcam sites then gave birth to more online modes of video sharing, from vlogs (video blogs) to the more recent innovations like social media stories, InstagramTV and Facebook live.

These formats can be seen as direct descendants of reality TV in many ways. Social media stories and vlogs directly draw upon the same techniques as video diary formats, such as people speaking directly to camera in a head-and-shoulders shot. However, there is often more playfulness at work on social media through the addition of emoji, stickers, slogans and filters that mark this content out as distinctive from the more professional and polished style of broadcast television (although more recent reality shows like *Dinner Date* and *Hot Property* do make use of emoji and slogans, they are still the minority at the time of writing).

In addition, television is constrained by broadcasting timeslots – typically ranging from 45 minutes to three hours in the case of reality shows. Social media content, on the other hand, can vary in length. Whilst online video and podcasts *can* run for several hours, internet content in general tends to be shorter than television content – most obviously in the case of a single image shared on Instagram or SnapChat, but even a YouTube video tends to be only a few minutes long.

Length is not the only difference between television and content designed for the internet. The format of a daily vlog, for instance, offers less in the way of storylining, drama and editing than reality TV, and focuses more on mundane rituals like cleaning and shopping. Even when using high-end equipment, YouTubers, for example, can deliberately make content appear more 'amateur' through leaving in mistakes in delivery and editing – what Jerslev (2016) terms 'performances of spontaneity' (p. 5423). This editing echoes that of reality TV in deliberately including things that went 'wrong' as a claim to the veracity of the video evidence.

Amateurness is further performed online through the lack of broadcasting conventions such as indicating when an advert break is coming (online videos still have advert 'breaks', but creators do not have control over where these come, so they interrupt the flow more than scheduled break points in TV). The way presenters address the audience offers a greater perception of intimacy and being part of a community than is found on mainstream television. Even when YouTube channels are reaching an audience of millions, they often adopt the same mode of address as if they were reaching a handful of viewers, by mentioning specific viewers by name or addressing specific fan comments and concerns.

FAME, IMAGE AND SELF-PRESENTATION ONLINE

The idea of the 'authentic' is as important to social media as it is to reality television. And, as reality performers balance a performance of both 'amateurness' and 'celebrity', so do internet stars.

One of the key terms in the study of internet celebrity is *microcelebrity*, which Senft calls 'A new style of online performance in which people employ webcams, video, audio, blogs, and social networking sites to amp up their popularity among readers, viewers, and those to whom they are linked online' (Senft, 2008, p. 25) and 'A new way to perform the self that combines the visual techniques of corporate branding with distribution technologies of the Internet' (Senft, 2009). Microcelebrity extends the idea of 'ordinary celebrity' by saying that the intersection between ordinary and celebrity does not rely on traditional media like TV. Instead, everyone can engage in celebrity-like practices and think 'about the self as a persona presented to an audience of fans' (Marwick, 2010).

However, there is a distinction between microcelebrity as a practice all users can engage in and internet, or online, celebrity as a status conferred on those with a level of 'fame' beyond their immediate circle, who are in some ways closer to reality stars in the size of their fame (Abidin, 2018; Giles, 2018). And, as with reality TV, the select few who have 'made it' stand as evidence that 'anyone' can be famous, rich and influential. This entices more people to engage in forms of unpaid labour (such as promoting brands in exchange for products or writing for websites 'for exposure') on the neo-liberal promise that they, too, can be noticed and achieve rewards if only they perform well enough.

There is a perception that internet stars, like reality stars, should remain in touch with their amateur, humble, roots in order to appear authentic. Even if they wear the visible markers of fame and success in the form of equipment, clothing, home décor, whitened teeth and styled hair, there should be a sense that their personality, their essential character, is the same as the person the audience first fell in love with.

Crystal Abidin (2018) describes the mechanisms and techniques by which these stars demonstrate this authenticity as 'calibrated amateurism' and 'performative authenticity' (p. 91). For example, direct address to the audience (Tolson, 2010), evidence of domestic life (e.g. doorbells ringing, pets making noise or wandering into shot) or leaving in editing errors.

For more traditional celebrities, too, social media's so-called 'authenticity' is a key part of its appeal. Because many celebrities post as themselves, there is a sense by which social media offers audiences direct access to the 'authentic' experiences of stars, bypassing 'cultural intermediaries' (Rojek, 2001) like agents, producers, journalists and PRs. The potential, then, is for celebrities to have a sense of authenticity that can add some credibility to their brand:

> *for some celebrities, Twitter seems to offer an opportunity to bypass even their own agents and public relations staff, breaking free of corporate image-management in order to gain the reward of direct communication with their fans, as well as some useful street-cred as a celebrity who has 'bucked the system' and undermined the publicity process by speaking honestly and directly to their fans. (Turner, 2014, p. 75)*

This process also offers celebrities potential access to audience opinion without having it pre-filtered for them, and the power to bestow favour on certain fans by sharing their content or answering their questions (Marwick & boyd, 2011).

By witnessing stars' private moments, thoughts and opinions that might previously have been private, social media acts as a way of potentially revealing the 'backstage' version of celebrity presentation, in similar ways to some celebrity reality TV formats (see Chapter 5). As Marwick and boyd (2011) observe, 'Reality TV popularized a behind-the-scenes, self-conscious examination of celebrity construction; online, this goes one step further' (p. 141).

It is sometimes surprising which stars do and do not offer self-revelatory content on social media. The Kardashian/Jenner clan, whose reality shows offer a sense of the whole front and backstage operation, offers surprisingly little in the way of personal revelation on their social media. They release snippets of their lives on social media (including, famously, the first photo of Kim Kardashian and Kanye West's wedding), and occasionally share opinions on politics and news events, but they primarily use social media to drive audiences to their merchandise or their other sites of stardom such as magazine interviews or TV shows.

INTERNET CELEBRITY MEETS REALITY CELEBRITY

As with reality television stars, traditional media (and audiences) offer strong opinions on who is, or is not, deserving of the spoils of fame. Citizen journalists, influencers, YouTubers and other internet celebrities have often been criticised by mainstream media for having dubious credentials, lacking in talent, making money for doing very little and for promoting undesirable lifestyles, beliefs or behaviours to their audiences (see Deller & Murphy, 2019; Giles, 2018; Rettberg, 2013; Senft, 2013).

Perhaps surprisingly, given the similar accusations levelled at it (see Chapter 2), reality television has also taken part in judging the validity of internet celebrities, whilst simultaneously exploiting their fame in the hope of attracting young audiences away from social media and back to traditional television. There are shows dedicated to those who have online fame (e.g. *Rich Kids of Instagram, Rise of the Superstar Vloggers*). However, these programmes are rarely celebratory and often approach online fame with a degree of scepticism.

Reality shows are now beginning to cast people who already have a sizeable internet following. These people not only potentially bring an audience with them but have also honed skills of communication, self-presentation, marketing and image management that can serve them well in the television environment. However, the fact that it is still more common to see internet celebrities on civilian reality shows rather than celebrity editions says something interesting about the hierarchies of fame.

FROM *BIG BROTHER* TO *THE CIRCLE*

To bring us back to where we started this chapter, reality show *The Circle* (which has several international versions forthcoming, in conjunction with Netflix) offers an interesting example of reality TV's approach to the internet. It is an unorthodox take on a fly-on-the-wall-meets-social-experiment format. Several individuals move into an unused apartment block, each in a different flat, and, sealed off from one another and the rest of the world (except for the production team and deliveries of food, et cetera on a daily basis), they meet, bond and rate one another over a social media platform created for the show.

In *The Circle* (the name of the platform as well as the show), participants engage in common social media activities: sharing daily updates, uploading profile pictures, messaging one another in 1–1 and group chats and taking part in games and challenges.

Part of the promotional gimmick is the idea that anybody could be anyone online – playing with the idea of 'catfishing', the process where someone pretends to be someone else online, often for the purposes of dating. The term was popularised by the film *Catfish* (dir. Henry Joost & Ariel Schuman, 2010), which spawned a spin-off MTV reality show of the same name, bringing together online 'couples' who have never previously met face to face to expose the 'reality' behind the internet personae.

In the first UK series of *The Circle* only a small number of participants operated as catfish – this number slightly increased in the second series (which began as this book went to press - the international editions have not yet begun). Three participants pretended to be somebody entirely different. A few others disguised aspects of themselves, such as their sexuality or age, whilst retaining their real names and using photographs of themselves. The majority, however, played a version of their true self, with the same age, interests, etc.

As contestants talked and bonded, they had to rate one another, using a star-rating mechanic that aped online review sites, with the lowest rated participants 'blocked' from the show. The star-rating process was very similar to that used in *Black Mirror*'s 'Nosedive' episode (where the social structure relies on achieving high ratings), something picked up on by many fans and journalists:

> The Circle *'is everything* Black Mirror *warned us about'. The new series is a little too mad for some viewers. (Edwards, 2018)*

The need for a high star rating led to participants constantly speculating over their strategies for posting and making connections, making overt not only the self-branding strategies we all engage in online, but the game playing aspect of reality television.

The strongest storyline of the series centred on eventual winner, Alex Hobern, who pretended to be a woman named Kate, using photographs of his girlfriend, Millie. In his intro VT, he discussed his rationale:

> The Circle *is the ultimate personality contest. And I was never very popular at school, so I've created the ultimate popular person.*

The Kate character tried to be friendly to everyone, but during the show's progression, became a target of hate from some other players for being 'bland', 'sitting on the fence' and potentially 'fake' – especially after other departing players were revealed to be catfish and suspicions grew – before being redeemed in the final vote as 'original' participants voted for each other over contenders who had entered the show later on. Kate/Alex's biggest storyline was a friendship built with non-catfish contestant, Dan. Dan's attempts to build a romantic liaison with Kate were rebuffed at every turn, with Alex frequently agonising over his deception and wanting Dan to know that their friendship bond was real.

The final episode of the show saw the four finalists meet face-to-face, and included the climax of the Dan/Kate storyline, where Dan reacted angrily to the revelation of Alex having catfished him, and Alex profusely apologised. Alex/Kate won the show, being voted most popular by fellow contestants AND the audience. What won the show for Alex from his housemates' point of view was his ability to be completely fake and have them believe in the persona of Kate, but from the audience's point of view, it was the real Alex and the self-consciousness, humour, doubt and wit he displayed that gave him the victory.

Despite using the concept of a social network the members of *The Circle* were treated more like *Big Brother* stars – disconnected from the rest of the internet and the world. They were only able to interact with one another, and only received information from the outside world in the form of a daily news story delivered by producers for comment, or the occasional mention of viewer comments and polls.

For all its claims to be a reality show for the social media age, *The Circle* was curiously limited in its use of social media to enhance the audience experience. An app allowed viewers to vote, but offered little in the way of enhanced content – only really offering a handful of short post-eviction interview clips from evictees, and occasional previews of the next episode. Their social media presence offered preview clips and memes of key moments, but nothing particularly distinctive or original that would incite audiences to follow the show through these other technologies.

The participants themselves, however, have capitalised on the possibilities of social media to try and sustain their fame beyond the show. Dan and Alex took their story to social media immediately after the show, sharing Instagram and Twitter posts of their post-show conversations to try and clear the air, eventually not only becoming friends (the happy ending viewers, and Alex, wanted) but also starting their own YouTube and podcast series. Other participants similarly exploited the connections made in the show on their social media to continue their stories. As I put the finishing touches to this chapter, over 6 months since the show ended, I have just seen a video featuring Alex and fellow finalist Freddie pop up in my Instagram feed!

The Circle offers an intriguing example of the state of reality television in the social media age. It knowingly plays with the ideas of 'reality', performance and being 'genuine'. As one of the central aims of the show is that 'they can go to extremes to be liked, changing their age, appearance, even their whole identity' (voiceover, S1E1, 2018), then we could argue that playing a character *is* playing the game authentically. Catfishes still revealed their own personalities and preferences in some of their interactions, and those playing 'themselves' still made choices about self-presentation in order to maximise their popularity. The humour present in the show's voiceovers, tasks and the participants' own behaviours and monologuing situates it as a very 'meta' programme, fully aware of the tropes of reality television, even as it reinforces them.

The Circle, like *Catfish*, hints at an interesting dynamic between television and social media, where television presents itself as the arbiter of truth, the place that exposes the lies and deception of social media.

THE FUTURE OF REALITY TELEVISION

So, what about the future of reality television? It is likely that we will continue to see reality television capitalise on developments within social media technologies. Whether or not this will extend to creating reality shows for virtual and augmented reality technologies is less clear. We may see them used within programmes (as in BBC Two show *Your Home Made Perfect*, where participants are shown VR home makeovers before committing to renovations) but any further experimentation will depend on the domestic uptake of these technologies and whether they can enhance the TV experience rather than being a gimmick.

We are likely to see the continued trend towards streaming services, meaning that some formats will move further away from being watched live (although live broadcast event TV does not look to be going anywhere for the foreseeable future). Given popular culture's tendency towards nostalgia, I would be surprised if we do not see more reality show archives being made available via streaming services, more 'where are they now' specials and internet content, and more anniversary formats – especially as popular franchises approach 20th and 25th anniversaries. Reboots will probably increase, bolstered by the success of *Changing Rooms* in Australia and *Queer Eye* on Netflix (although Channel 4's recent *Shipwrecked* relaunch bombed, so there is no guarantee reboots will work).

What we are most likely to see in the future is more hybridisation; in areas of celebrity, hybridisation between the ordinary, the superstar and the micro-celebrity; in areas of distribution and consumption, hybridisation of technologies and modes of engagement; and in the content of shows, a hybridisation of traditional values and newer, more challenging ideas.

The focus on ethics in reality television is not, I imagine, going away anytime soon, and reflects a broader attention to the ethics of television and the media. However, as is often the case with such panics, we may just see a few scapegoats being disciplined rather than a sea change of the fundamental issues of exploitation surrounding the industry.

Whatever its futures, the continued endurance and popularity of reality television suggests that, far from being an ephemeral phenomenon, it is as central to the television landscape as documentary, sitcom or news and will not be going away anytime soon.

NOTES

1. https://www.dailystar.co.uk/tv/x-factor-2017-uk-fake-17029338

2. https://twitter.com/iamlewisdean?lang=en

REFERENCES

Abidin, C. (2018). *Internet celebrity: Understanding fame online*. Bingley: Emerald Publishing.

Agius, N. (2016). 'Greedy' Great British Bake Off slammed as 'disgraceful' by stunned celebrities and former contestants. *Mirror*. Retrieved from https://www.mirror.co.uk/tv/tv-news/greedy-great-british-bake-slammed-8823297

Allen, K., & Mendick, H. (2012). Keeping it real? Social class, young people and 'authenticity' in reality TV. *Sociology*, *47*(3), 460–476. https://doi.org/10.1177/0038038512448563

Andrejevic, M. (2004). *Reality TV: The work of being watched*. Lanham, MD: Rowman & Littlefield.

Andrejevic, M. (2008). Watching television without pity: The productivity of online fans. *Television & New Media*, *9*(1), 24–46. https://doi.org/10.1177/1527476407307241

Barron, L. (2015). *Celebrity cultures: An introduction*. Los Angeles, CA: Sage.

Bell-Jordan, K. E. (2008). Black white and a survivor of the real world: Constructions of race on reality TV. *Critical Studies in Media Communication*, *25*(4), 353–372, DOI: 10.1080/15295030802327725

Bennett, J. (2011). *Television personalities: Stardom and the small screen*. London: Routledge.

Bignell, J. (2005). *Big Brother: Reality TV in the twenty-first century*. Basingstoke: Palgrave Macmillan.

Biltereyst, D. (2004). Reality TV, troublesome pictures and panics: Reappraising the public controversy around reality TV in Europe. In S. Holmes & D. Jermyn (Eds.), *Understanding reality television* (pp. 91–110). London; New York: Routledge.

Biressi, A. (2011). The virtuous circle: social entrepreneurship and welfare programming in the UK. In H. Wood & B. Skeggs (Eds.), *Reality Television and Class* (pp. 144–155). London: British Film Institute.

Biressi, A., & Nunn, H. (2005). *Reality TV: Realism and revelation*. London: Wallflower.

Blackmon, M. (2017). Tiffany Richardson doesn't need you to root for her any more. *BuzzFeed*. Retrieved from https://www.buzzfeed.com/michaelblackmon/we-were-rooting-for-you-we-were-all-rooting-for-you

Bonner, F. (2003). *Ordinary television: Analyzing popular TV*. London: Sage.

Bonner, F. (2011). *Personality presenters: Television's intermediaries with viewers*. Farnham: Ashgate.

Bonner, F. (2013). Celebrity, work and the reality-talent show: Strictly come dancing/dancing with the stars. *Celebrity Studies, 4*(2), 169–181. doi:10.1080/19392397.2013.791038

Booth, P. (2010). *Digital Fandom*. New York, NY: Peter Lang.

Bourdieu, P. (1984). *Distinction: A social critique of the judgement of taste*. Cambridge, MA: Harvard University Press.

Bricker, T. (2018). How much reality tv contestants actually make (if anything). *E!* Retrieved from https://www.eonline.com/uk/news/976257/ how-much-reality-tv-contestants-actually-make-if-anything

Brooker, C. (2008). Reality Bites. *The Guardian.* Retrieved from https://www.theguardian.com/film/2008/oct/18/horror-channel4

Brookstein, S. (2015). *Getting Over the X.* Leicester: Matador.

Bruns, A. (2011). Tweeting at the TV: Some Observations on #GoBackSBS. *Mapping Online.*

Campbell, M. (2007). The mocking mockumentary and the ethics of irony. *Taboo, 11*(1), 53–62. doi:10.31390/ taboo.11.1.08

Cashmore, E. (2014). *Celebrity culture.* Abingdon: Routledge.

CBS (2019) Big Brother Live Feeds. *CBS.* Retrieved from https://www.cbs.com/shows/big_brother/live_feed/

Channel 4. (2018). *Annual Report 2018.* Retrieved from https://annualreport.channel4.com/assets/ downloads/203_30612_Channel4_AR2018-accessible-v2.pdf

Cleary, K. (2016). Misfitting and hater blocking: A feminist disability analysis of the extraordinary body on reality television. *Disability Studies Quarterly, 36*(4). https://doi. org/10.18061/dsq.v36i4.5442

Cohen, S. (2002). *Folk Devils and Moral Panics: The Creation of the Mods and the Rockers.* (3rd ed.) London: Routledge.

Corner, J. (2004). Afterword: Framing the new. In S. Holmes & D. Jermyn (Eds.), *Understanding reality television* (pp. 290–299). London; New York: Routledge.

Couldry, N. (2003). *Media rituals: A critical approach*. London: Routledge.

Couldry, N. (2009). Media rituals from Durkheim on religion to Jade Goody on religious toleration. In C. Deacy & E. Arweck (Eds.), *Exploring religion and the media in a sacred age* (pp. 43–70). London: Ashgate.

Damshenas, S. (2019). Here's how former *Drag Race* contestants reacted to the All Stars 4 finale. *Gay Times*. Retrieved from https://www.gaytimes.co.uk/culture/118640/heres-how-former-drag-race-contestants-reacted-to-the-all-stars-4-finale/

Dauncey, H. (1996). French 'Reality Television': More Than a Matter of Taste? *European Journal of Communication*, *11*(1), 83–106.

Davis, W. (2012). The reality anatomist: Chris Lilley and the mockumentary form. *Screen Education*, (67), 94–102.

DCMS. (2019). Committee announces inquiry into reality TV. *UK Parliament Website*. Retrieved from https://www.parliament.uk/business/committees/committees-a-z/commons-select/digital-culture-media-and-sport-committee/news/reality-tv-inquiry-launch-17-19/

Deery, J. (2015) *Reality TV*. Cambridge: Polity.

Deller, R. A. (2011). Twittering on: Audience research and participation using twitter. participations, volume 8, issue 1. Retrieved from http://www.participations.org/Volume%;208/Issue%201/deller.htm

Deller, R. A. (2012a). *Faith in view: Religion and spirituality in factual British TV 2000–09*. PhD thesis. Retrieved from http://shura.shu.ac.uk/5654/

Deller, R. A. (2012b). Gender performance in *American Idol, Pop Idol* and *The X Factor*. In K. Zwaan & J. de

Bruin (Eds.), *Adapting idols: Authenticity, identity and performance in a global television format* (pp. 181–194). Farnham: Ashgate.

Deller, R. A. (2014a). Religion as makeover: Reality, lifestyle and spiritual transformation. *International Journal of Cultural Studies*, *18*(3), 291–303. https://doi.org/10.1177/1367877913513687

Deller, R. A. (2014b). The Art of Neighbours gaming: Facebook, fan-crafted games and humour. *Intensities: The Journal of Cult Media*, *7*, 97–106.

Deller, R. A. (2016). Star image, celebrity reality television and the fame cycle. *Celebrity Studies*, *7*(3), 373–389. doi:10.1080/19392397.2015.1133313

Deller, R. A., & Murphy, K. (2019). 'Zoella hasn't really written a book, she's written a cheque': Mainstream media representations of YouTube celebrities. *European Journal of Cultural Studies*. https://doi.org/10.1177/1367549419861638

Dixon, E. (2018). 'Great British Bake Off' Producer Says Moving To Channel 4 Saved The Show. *Bustle*. Retrieved from https://www.bustle.com/p/great-british-bake-off-producer-says-moving-to-channel-4-saved-the-show-13187556

Dover, C., & Hill, A. (2007). Mapping genres: Broadcaster and audience perceptions of makeover television. In D. Heller (Ed.), *Makeover television: Realities remodelled* (pp. 23–38). London: I.B.Tauris.

Dovey, J. (2000). *Freakshow : First person media and factual television*. London: Pluto.

Dyer, R. (1979). *Stars*. London: BFI.

Dyer, R. (1986). *Heavenly bodies: Film stars and society*. London: BFI.

Earnshaw, T. (2017). *Ghostwatch* writer Stephen Volk remembers the drama that terrified millions. *Examiner Live*. Retrieved from https://www.examinerlive.co.uk/news/tv/ghostwatch-writer-stephen-volk-remembers-13833560

Edwards, C. (2018). Channel 4's social media-based reality show *The Circle* "is everything *Black Mirror* warned us about". *Digital Spy*. Retrieved from https://www.digitalspy.com/tv/reality-tv/a866508/channel-4-reality-show-the-circle-black-mirror/

Endemol. (2019). About us. *EndemolShine Group*. Retrieved from https://www.endemolshinegroup.com/about/

Essany, M. (2008). *Reality check: The business and art of producing reality TV*. Oxford: Focal.

Foucault, M. (1976). *The history of sexuality, vol. 1: The will to knowledge*. London: Penguin

Foucault, M. (1977). *Discipline and punish: The birth of the prison* (translated by A. Sheridan). London: Penguin.

Friedman, M. (2014). Here comes a lot of judgment: Honey Boo Boo as a site of reclamation and resistance. *Journal of Popular Television*, 2(1) 77–95.

Fry, C. (2019). A Fire Burned At The Old Big Brother House Yesterday, 'Cos Nothing Is Sacred'. *Pedestrian*. Retrieved from https://www.pedestrian.tv/news/big-brother-house-fire-2019/

Gabriel, S., Paravati, E., Green, M. C., & Flomsbee, J. (2018). From Apprentice to President: The Role of Parasocial Connection in the Election of Donald Trump. *Social Psychological and Personality*

Science, *9*(3), 299–307. Retrieved from https://doi.
org/10.1177/1948550617722835

Gamson, J. (2014). "It's been a while since I've seen, like
straight people": Queer visibility in the age of postnetwork
reality television. In L. Ouellette (Ed.), *A companion to
reality television* (pp. 227–246). Chichester: Wiley Blackwell.

Geiringer, D. (2019). What *Love Island* can teach us about
the history of love. *The Conversation*. Retrieved from
https://theconversation.com/what-love-island-can-tell-us-
about-the-history-of-love-119751

Ghattas, M. (2012). *Superstar* and Middle Eastern political
identities. In K. Zwaan & J. de Bruin (Eds.), *Adapting idols:
Authenticity, identity and performance in a global television
format* (pp. 123–134). Farnham: Ashgate.

Gilbert, A. (2019). Hatewatch with me: Anti-fandom as
performative consumption. In M. Click (Ed.), *Dislike, hate,
and anti-fandom in the digital age* (pp. 62–80). New York, NY:
New York University Press.

Giles, D. (2018). *Twenty-first century celebrity: Fame in
digital culture*. Bingley: Emerald Publishing.

Gillan, J. (2004). From Ozzie Nelson to Ozzy Osbourne: The
genesis and development of the reality (star) sitcom. In S.
Holmes & D. Jermyn (Eds.), *Understanding reality television*
(pp. 54–70). London, New York: Routledge.

Goddard, P. (2018). Debating distinctiveness: How useful a
concept is it in measuring the impact and value of the BBC?
In D. Freedman, & V. Goblot (Eds.), A future for public
service television (pp. 165–169). London: Goldsmiths Press.

Gray, J. (2003). New audiences, new textualities: Anti-fans
and non-fans. *International Journal of Cultural Studies*, *6*(1),
64–81. https://doi.org/10.1177/1367877903006001004

Gray, J. (2005). Antifandom and the Moral Text: *Television Without Pity* and Textual Dislike. *American Behavioral Scientist*, 48(7), 840–858. Rerieved from https://doi.org/10.1177/0002764204273171

Gray, J. (2010). *Show sold separately: Promos, spoilers, and other media paratexts*. New York, NY: NYU Press.

Grindstaff, L. (1997). Producing trash, class, and the money shot: A behind-the-scenes account of daytime TV talk shows. In S. Hinerman & J. Lull (Eds.), *Media scandals: Morality and desire in the popular culture marketplace* (pp. 164–202). Cambridge: Polity.

Grindstaff, L. (2012). Reality TV and the production of 'ordinary celebrity': Notes from the field. *Berkeley Journal of Sociology*, 56, 22–40.

Hall, A. (2006). Viewers' perceptions of reality programs. *Communication Quarterly*, 54(2), 191–211. DOI: 10.1080/01463370600650902

Hall, S. (1973). *Encoding and decoding in the television discourse*. Birmingham: Centre for Contemporary Cultural Studies.

Hall, S. M., & Holmes, H. (2017). Making do and getting by? Beyond a romantic politics of austerity and crisis. *Discover Society*. https://discoversociety.org/2017/05/02/making-do-and-getting-by-beyond-a-romantic-politics-of-austerity-and-crisis/

Hawkins, G. (2001). The ethics of television. *International Journal of Cultural Studies*, 4, 432–426.

Hearn, A. (2016). Trump's "reality" hustle. *Television & New Media*, 17(7), 656–659. doi:10.1177/1527476416652699

Hight, C. (2004). 'It isn't always Shakespeare, but it's genuine': Cinema's commentary on documentary hybrids. In S. Holmes & D. Jermyn (Eds.), *Understanding reality television* (pp. 233–251). London, New York: Routledge.

Hight, C. (2010). *Television mockumentary: Reflexivity, satire and a call to play*. Manchester: Manchester University Press.

Hill, A. (2005). *Reality TV: Audiences and popular factual television*. London: Routledge.

Hill, A. (2007). *Restyling factual TV audiences and news, documentary and reality genres*. London: Routledge.

Hill, A. (2011). *Paranormal media*. London: Routledge.

Hill, A. (2019). *Media experiences: Reality TV, producers and audiences*. Abingdon: Routledge.

Hill, A., Weibull, L., & Nilsson, A. (2005). *Audiences and factual and reality television in Sweden*. JIBS. Jönköping. Retrieved from http://edit.center.hj.se/download/18.2eec38e0133eaafba4a80002984/1520583406773/audiences.pdf

Holmes, S. (2006). It's a jungle out there!: The game of fame in celebrity reality TV. In S. Holmes & S. Redmond (Eds.), *Framing celebrity: New directions in celebrity culture* (pp. 45–66). Abingdon: Routledge.

Holmes, S. (2009). Jade's back and this time she's famous: Narratives of celebrity in the Celebrity bigbrother 'race' row. *Entertainment and Sports Law Journal*, 7(1). Retrieved from http://www2.warwick.ac.uk/fac/soc/law/elj/eslj/issues/volume7/number1/holmes

Holmes, S., & Jermyn, D. (Eds.). (2004). *Understanding reality television*. London, New York: Routledge.

Horgan-Wallace, A. (2009). *Aisleyne: Surviving guns, gangs and glamour*. Edinburgh: Mainstream.

ITV. (2019). Statement regarding the Jeremy Kyle Show. *ITV*. Retrieved from https://www.itv.com/presscentre/press-releases/statement-itv-regarding-jeremy-kyle-show

Jablonski, S. (2008). Charlie Brooker talks to us about Dead Set. *Den of Geek*. Retrieved from https://www.denofgeek.com/tv/19682/charlie-brooker-talks-to-us-about-dead-set

Jacobs, S. (2007). Big Brother, Africa is watching. *Media, Culture & Society*, *29*(6), 851–868. https://doi.org/10.1177/0163443707081691

Jenkins, H. (2006). *Convergence culture: Where old and new media collide*. London; New York: New York University Press.

Jenkins, H., Ford, S., & Green, J. B. (2013). *Spreadable media: Creating value and meaning in a networked culture*. New York, NY: New York University Press.

Jensen, T. (2014). Welfare commonsense, poverty porn and doxosophy. *Sociological Research Online*, *19*(3), 1–7. https://doi.org/10.5153/sro.3441

Jerslev, A. (2016). In the Time of the Microcelebrity: Celebrification and the YouTuber Zoella. *International Journal of Communication*, *10*, 5233–5251.

Jones, J. (2003). Show your real face: A fan study of the UK big brother transmissions (2000, 2001, 2002). Investigating the boundaries between notions of consumers and producers of factual television. *New Media & Society*, *5*(3), 400–421.

Kaur, N. (2007). *Big Brother: The inside story*. London: Virgin.

Kavka, M. (2012). *Reality TV*. Edinburgh: Edinburgh University Press.

Kilborn, R. W. (2010). *Taking the long view: A study of longitudinal documentary*. Manchester: Manchester University Press.

Kilborn, R. W., & Izod, J. (1997). *An introduction to television documentary: Confronting reality*. Manchester: University Press.

Knowledge Agency/Ofcom. (2019). *Adults' Media Lives 2019*. Retrieved from https://www.ofcom.org.uk/__data/assets/pdf_file/0022/149251/adults-media-lives-report.pdf

Kraidy, M. (2011). *Reality television and Arab Politics*. Cambridge: Cambridge University Press.

Kraidy, M. (2014). Reality Television from *Big Brother* to the Arab Uprisings. In L. Ouellette (Ed.), *A companion to reality television* (pp. 541–556). Chichester: Wiley Blackwell.

Lewis, T. (2009). *TV transformations: Revealing the makeover show*. London: Routledge.

Lovelock, M. W. (2016). *Interrogating the politics of LGBT celebrity in British reality television*. PhD thesis. Retrieved from https://ueaeprints.uea.ac.uk/63063/1/Thesis_final.pdf

Lundy, L. K., Ruth, A. M., & Park, T. D. (2008). Simply irresistible: Reality TV consumption patterns. *Communication Quarterly*, *56*(2), 208–225. doi:10.1080/01463370802026828

Mallett, R. (2010). Claiming comedic immunity: Or, what do you get when you cross contemporary British comedy with disability? *Review of Disability Studies*, *6*(3), 5–14.

Maloney, C. (2018). *Wildcard*. Newcastle: Wild Wolf
Publishing.

Marwick, A. (2010). *Status update: Celebrity, publicity and
self-branding in Web 2.0* (PhD thesis). New York, NY: New
York University. Retrieved from https://search.proquest.com/
openview/afee20b21867fe41e81de73d860c7359/1?pq-origsi
te=gscholar&cbl=18750&diss=y

Marwick, A. E., & Boyd, D. (2010). I tweet honestly, I
tweet passionately: Twitter users, context collapse, and the
imagined audience. *New Media & Society, 13*(1), 114–133.
https://doi.org/10.1177/1461444810365313

Marwick, A. E., & Boyd, D. (2011). To see and be seen:
Celebrity practice on twitter. *Convergence: The International
Journal of Research into New Media Technologies, 17*(2),
139–158. doi:10.1177/1354856510394539

Mayer, V. (2014). Cast-aways: The plights and pleasures of
reality casting and production studies. In L. Ouellette (Ed.),
A companion to reality television (pp. 57–73). Chichester:
Wiley Blackwell.

McCrum, M. (2000). *Castaway 2000: The full, inside story
of the major BBC TV series*. London: Ebury.

Michelle, C. (2009). (Re)contextualising audience receptions
of reality TV. *Participations: Journal of Audience and
Reception Studies, 6*(1), 137–170.

Morreale, J. (2003). Revisiting "The Osbournes":
The hybrid reality sitcom. *Journal of Film and Video,
55*(1), 3–15.

Nabi, R. L., Biely, E. N., Morgan, S. J., & Stitt, C. R. (2003).
Reality-based television programming and the psychology of
its appeal. *Media Psychology, 5*(4), 303–330. doi:10.1207/
S1532785XMEP0504_01

Oakes, O. (2019). Is the decline in young TV audiences accelerating? *Campaign*. Retrieved from https://www.campaignlive.co.uk/article/decline-young-tv-audiences-accelerating/1578795

Ofcom. (2016). *Adults' Media Lives 2016: A qualitative study. Wave 12 Summary Report*. Retrieved from https://www.ofcom.org.uk/__data/assets/pdf_file/0021/102756/adults-media-lives-2016.pdf

Ofcom. (2018). Most complained about TV programmes of 2018. *Ofcom*. Retrieved from https://www.ofcom.org.uk/about-ofcom/latest/media/media-releases/2018/most-complained-about-tv-programmes-of-2018

Osbourne, S. (2005). *Extreme: My autobiography*. London: Time Warner Books.

Ouellette, L. (2016). The Trump show. *Television & New Media*, *17*(7), 647–650. https://doi.org/10.1177/1527476416652695

Palmer, A. (2018). *Great British Bake Off*: Bullying BBC wanted to let show crumble and die, claims producer. *Express*. Retrieved from https://www.express.co.uk/showbiz/tv-radio/1048381/Great-British-Bakeoff-UK-TV-BBC.

Papacharissi, Z., & Mendelson, A. L. (2007). An exploratory study of reality appeal: Uses and gratifications of reality TV shows. *Journal of Broadcasting & Electronic Media*, *51*(2), 355–370. doi:10.1080/08838150701307152

Payne, R., (2009). Dancing with the ordinary: Masculine celebrity performance on Australian TV. *Continuum: Journal of Media & Cultural Studies*, *23*(3), 295–306.

Pidd, H. (2014). How Grimsby went to war with Channel 4 over *Skint*. *The Guardian*. Retrieved from https://www.theguardian.com/commentisfree/2014/apr/01/grimsby-channel-4-skint-documentary-benefits-street

Publics. Retrieved from http://mappingonlinepublics.
net/2011/07/07/tweeting-at-the-tv-some-observations-
on-gobacksbs/

Radio Times Team. (2011). Charlie Brooker previews black
mirror episode two – 15 million merits. *Radio Times*. Retrieved
from https://www.radiotimes.com/news/2011-12-09/charlie-
brooker-previews-black-mirror-episode-two-15-million-merits/

Rahman, M. (2008). Jade's confession: Racism and the
dialectics of celebrity. *Social Semiotics*, *18*(2), 133–148.
doi:10.1080/10350330802002143

Raisborough, J. (2011). *Lifestyle media and the formation of
the self*. Basingstoke: Palgrave Macmillan.

Raisborough, J., Frith, H., & Klein, O. (2013). Media
and class-making: What lessons are learnt when
a celebrity chav dies? *Sociology*, *47*(2), 251–266.
doi:10.1177/0038038512444813

Redden, G. (2007). Makeover morality and consumer
culture. In D. Heller (Ed.), *Makeover television: Realities
remodelled* (pp. 150–164). London: I.B. Tauris.

Rettberg, J. W. (2013). *Blogging*. 2nd ed. Cambridge: Polity.

Richards, J. (2019). Let Us Revisit The Empty, Rotting
Carcass Of The Iconic 'Big Brother' House. *Junkee*. Retrieved
from https://junkee.com/big-brother-australia-house/207336

Richardson, N. (2018). The invisibles: Disability, sexuality
and new strategies of enfreakment. In C. Smith, F. Attwood,
& B. McNair (Eds.), *The Routledge companion to media,
sex and sexuality* (pp. 328–339). London: Routledge.

Ringrose, J., & Walkerdine, V. (2008). Regulating The
Abject. *Feminist Media Studies*, *8*(3), 227–246. Retrieved
from https://doi.org/10.1080/14680770802217279

Ritchie, J. (2000). *Big Brother: The official unseen story*. London: Channel 4.

Robinson, A. (2018). Here's how much people actually get paid to go on reality TV. *Digital Spy*. Retrieved from https://www.digitalspy.com/tv/reality-tv/a867564/reality-tv-pay-wages/

Rojek, C. (2001). *Celebrity*. London: Reaktion.

Ross, A. (2014). Reality television and the political economy of amateurism. In L. Ouellette (Ed.), *A companion to reality television* (pp. 29–39). Chichester: Wiley Blackwell.

Runswick-Cole, K., & Goodley, D. (2015b). DisPovertyPorn: And the dis/ability paradox. *Disability & Society, 30*(4), 645–649.

Sconce, J. (2004). See you in hell Johnny Bravo! In S. Murray & L. Oullette (Eds.), *Reality TV: Remaking television culture* (pp. 251–267). New York, NY: New York University Press.

Seiter, E. (1990). Making distinctions in TV audience research: Case study of a troubling interview. *Cultural Studies, 4*(1), 61–84, DOI: 10.1080/09502389000490051

Sender, K. (2012). *The makeover: Reality television and reflexive audiences*. New York, NY: New York University Press.

Sender, K., & Sullivan, M. (2009). Epidemics of will, failures of self-esteem: Responding to fat bodies in The Biggest Loser and What Not to Wear. In T. Lewis (Ed.), *TV transformations: Revealing the makeover show* (pp. 133–144). London: Routledge.

Senft, T. M. (2008). *Camgirls: Celebrity and community in the age of social networks*. New York, NY: Oxford: P. Lang.

Senft, T. M. (2009). The case of online micro-celebrity gangsta flirtation. Retrieved from http://tsenft.livejournal.com/405196.html

Senft, T. M. (2013). Microcelebrity and the branded self. In J. Hartley, J. Burgess, & A. Bruns (Eds.), *A companion to new media dynamics* (pp. 346–354). Oxford: Wiley-Blackwell.

Shattuc, J. M. (1997). *The talking cure: TV talk shows and women*. London: Routledge.

Shifman, L. (2014). *Memes in digital culture*. Cambridge, MA: The MIT Press.

Singh, S., & Kretschmer, M. (2012). Strategic behaviour in the international exploitation of TV formats: A case study of the *Idols* format. In K. Zwaan & J. de Bruin (Eds.), *Adapting idols: Authenticity, identity and performance in a global television format* (pp. 11–26). Farnham: Ashgate.

Skeggs, B., Thumim, N., & Wood, H. (2008). 'Oh goodness, I am watching reality TV': How methods make class in audience research. *European Journal of Cultural Studies*, *11*(1), 5–24. doi:10.1177/1367549407084961

Skeggs, B., & Wood, H. (2012). *Reacting to reality television: Performance, audience and value*. London: Routledge.

Smith, A. (2019). 'How the hell did this get on tv?': Naked dating shows as the final taboo on mainstream TV. *European Journal of Cultural Studies*, *22*(5–6), 700–717. Retrieved from https://doi.org/10.1177/1367549419847107

Spencer, R. (2019). TELLY DEATH TOLL: *Love Island*'s Mike Thalassitis and Sophie Gradon's deaths among 38 suspected suicides linked to reality

TV shows worldwide. *The Sun*. Retrieved from
https://www.thesun.co.uk/tvandshowbiz/8705713/
love-island-mike-thalassitis-sophie-gradon-suicide-reality-tv/

Squires, C. R. (2014). *The post-racial mystique: Media and race in the twenty-first century*. New York: NYU Press.

Stephens, R. L. (2004). Socially soothing stories? Gender, race and class in TLC's *A Wedding Story* and *A Baby Story*. S. Holmes & D. Jermyn (Eds.), *Understanding reality television* (pp. 54–70). London, New York: Routledge.

Taylor, L. (2016). *A Taste for Gardening: Classed and Gendered Practices*. London: Routledge.

Tolson, A. (2010). A new authenticity? Communicative practices on YouTube. *Critical Discourse Studies*, 7(4), 277–289.

Turner, G. (2004). *Understanding celebrity* (1st ed). London: Sage.

Turner, G. (2006). The mass production of celebrity. *International Journal of Cultural Studies*, 9(2), 153–165. Doi:10.1177/1367877906064028

Turner, G. (2010) *Ordinary people and the media: the demotic turn*. London: Sage.

Turner, G. (2014). *Understanding celebrity* (2nd ed.). Los Angeles, CA: Sage.

Tyler, I. (2013). *Revolting subjects: Social abjection and resistance in neoliberal Britain*. London: Zed Books.

Tyler, I., & Bennett, B. (2010). 'Celebrity chav': Fame, femininity and social class. *European Journal of Cultural Studies*, 13(3), 375–393. doi:10.1177/1367549410363203

Weber, B. (2009). *Makeover TV: Selfhood, citizenship and celebrity*. Durham, NC: Duke University Press.

Wilson, J. A. (2014) Reality Television Celebrity: Star Consumption and Self-Production in Media Culture. In L. Ouellette (Ed.), *A Companion to Reality Television* (pp. 421–436). Chichester: Wiley Blackwell.

Woodford, D. (2013). Australian Reality TV on Twitter: A Two-Horse Race. *Mapping Online Publics*. Retrieved from https://mappingonlinepublics.net/2013/08/13/australian-reality-tv-on-twitter-a-two-horse-race/

Woods, R. (2017). *Ghostwatch*: The BBC spoof that duped a nation. *BBC News*. Retrieved from https://www.bbc.co.uk/news/uk-england-41740176

ACKNOWLEDGEMENTS

Thanks to all my interviewees for your time and honesty. To all at Emerald, thank you for your enthusiasm, patience and support, especially Alice Ford and Helen Beddow; to Philippa Grand for taking a punt on me in the first place. To all my interviewees for your time and honesty. To my friends from the *Lowculture* days, especially Paul Lang, Chris Rubery and my partner in crime, Steven Perkins. To all my colleagues and students at Sheffield Hallam University, past and present, especially Kathryn Murphy whose work on YouTube has given me plenty of thought, and, when I thought reality TV had gotten as weird as it could possibly get, alerted me to the existence of *Release the Hounds*. To all my friends and family, especially Feona Attwood for early chats that seeded some of this material. To Radio Sheffield who let me prattle on about TV to the poor folk of South Yorkshire at any given opportunity. To all my various physios, the hydro teams and especially to EW, for helping me keep body, mind and soul together(ish). To SM for your endless support, care and belief in me, and for helping me through the various times where I hit the wall. To Dragon – without you, I could never have written this, even if our relationship is hard work at times. And to everyone who has ever worked on, starred in, watched or written about reality shows. You have kept me entertained, amused, frustrated, annoyed and educated for many years, and this book literally would not exist without you!

FURTHER READING

GENERAL BOOKS ON REALITY TV

These books are for anyone looking for an overview of key histories, themes and developments in reality TV, from early works to more recent ones. Some are single-authored studies, others multi-authored volumes with a variety of topics inside. All are great if you want to get more insight into the phenomenon.

Biressi, A., & Nunn, H. (2005). *Reality TV: Realism and revelation*. London: Wallflower.

Deery, J. (2015). *Reality TV*. Cambridge: Polity.

Hill, A. (2019). *Media experiences: Reality TV, producers and audiences*. Abingdon: Routledge.

Holmes, S., & Jermyn, D. (Eds.). (2004). *Understanding reality television*. London: Routledge.

Kavka, M. (2012). *Reality TV*. Edinburgh: Edinburgh University Press.

Kraidy, M. M., & Sender, K. (Eds.). (2012). *The politics of reality television: Global perspectives*. London: Routledge.

Ouellette, L. (Ed.). (2014). *A companion to reality television*. Chichester: Wiley Blackwell.

BOOKS ON SPECIFIC THEMES AND FORMATS

These books are all a bit more specialised and look at key themes, genres and franchises for those wanting to dig a little deeper.

Lewis, T. (Ed.). (2009). *TV transformations: Revealing the makeover show*. London: Routledge.

Lovelock, M. (2019). *Reality TV and queer identities*. Basingstoke: Palgrave Macmillan.

Raisborough, J. (2011). *Lifestyle media and the formation of the self*. Basingstoke: Palgrave Macmillan.

Weber, B. (2009). *Makeover TV: Selfhood, citizenship and celebrity*. Durham, NC: Duke University Press.

Wood, H., & Skeggs, B. (Eds.). (2011). *Reality television and class*. London: BFI.

Zwaan, K., & de Bruin, J. (Eds.). (2012). *Adapting idols: Authenticity, identity and performance in a global television format*. Farnham: Ashgate.

BOOKS ON CELEBRITIES

Want to delve into the phenomenon of reality celebrity a little further? Then, any of these will give you plenty to think about in terms of histories and theories of fame, how reality stars fit into the celebrity world and how the new generation of internet celebrities fit into the celebrity sphere.

Abidin, C. (2018). *Internet celebrity: Understanding fame online*. Bingley: Emerald Publishing.

Barron, L. (2015). *Celebrity cultures: An introduction*. Los Angeles, CA: Sage.

Bennett, J. (2011). *Television personalities: Stardom and the small screen*. London: Routledge.

Giles, D. (2018). *Twenty-first century celebrity: Fame in digital culture*. Bingley: Emerald Publishing.

Redmond, S. (Ed.). (2011). *The star and celebrity confessional*. London: Routledge

Turner, G. (2010). *Ordinary people and the media: The demotic turn*. London: Sage.

INDEX